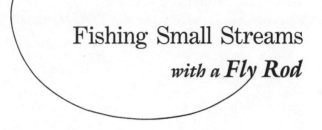

Fishing Small Streams
with a **Fly Rod**

Other Books by Charles R. Meck

Meeting and Fishing the Hatches
Pennsylvania Trout Streams and Their Hatches

Fishing Small Streams
with a Fly Rod

Charles R. Meck

The Countryman Press
Woodstock, Vermont

Library of Congress Cataloging-in Publication Data
Meck, Charles R.
    Fishing small streams with a fly rod/Charles R. Meck.
        p. cm.
    Includes index.
    ISBN 0-88150-201-4 (cloth ed.)
    ISBN 0-88150-202-2 (pbk ed.)
    1. Trout fishing. 2. Fly fishing. I. Title
    SH687.M348 1991
    799.1'755—dc20   91-13400 CIP

Printed in the United States

10 9 8 7 6 5 4

Published by The Countryman Press, PO Box 748, Woodstock, VT 05091
Distributed by W.W. Norton & Company, Inc., 500 Fifth Avenue,
    New York, NY 10110

Cover and text design by Virginia L. Scott

Line art on page 70, 72, 74, 75 copyright © 1991 by Patricia Witten.
Line art on pages 165, 166, 167, 168, 174 courtesy of Pennsylvania Fish
    Commission.

Photographs on pages 12, 22, 43, 59, 64 by Melvin Neidig; on pages 103
and 138 by Jeff L. Katherman; on page 93 by Greg Hoover.
All other photographs by the author.

To George W. Harvey, a great friend, a true teacher, and a fishing legend. He has taught me most of what I know about *Fishing Small Streams with a Fly Rod*.

Contents

Acknowledgments

Many people have assisted in preparing this manuscript. A special thanks to all of them. George Harvey and I have spent many days on small streams during the past couple years. He gave me many hours of informal instruction. Greg Hoover was always available when I needed him to identify mayflies, take photos, and tie up some special leaders. Thanks for all his help. Joe Dougherty, also an afficionado of small streams, has provided valuable information for the book. Mel Neidig was always available to take photos, and Tom Walsh and Terry Malloy, of Clearfield, Pennsylvania, showed me some of their favorite small streams. Thanks, also, to Ralph Frankenberger for developing photos for this book.

Mike Manfredo, Craig Shuman, and Don Rodriguez, of Fort Collins, Colorado, showed me some great Trico hatches on small Western waters. Ken Helfrich, of Springfield, Oregon, showed me plenty of trout on small streams in his state.

Thanks, also, to Robert Budd, of Altoona, and Andrew Leitzinger, of Collegeville, Pennsylvania. Both enjoy fly-fishing small streams.

Thanks to a quality company, Orvis, for its support.

Without the help of these people, *Fishing Small Streams with a Fly Rod* would never have been completed.

Introduction

WALT YOUNG, OF Altoona, Pennsylvania, affectionately calls it "ditch fishing." George Harvey and Joe Humphreys call it "brush fishing." Ralph Dougherty, of western Pennsylvania, has much more disdain for this type of fly-fishing. He claims you have no room above you and none to the right or left to cast a fly. Appropriately, he says, it's like fly-fishing in a tunnel. Joe Loue, in an article for the *Pennsylvania Angler*, called it fishing on "no-name streams."

George Harvey has fly-fished these trout streams all his life. He grew up on them. He fly-fishes dozens of these trout waters every year, and every new fly-fishing season he looks forward with great anticipation to another year.

What type of fishing waters are we talking about? What type of trout-fishing brings out this sharply diverse feeling from fly-fishermen? What collection of trout streams can one moment give you the feeling of total frustration and at another instant bring absolute satisfaction? For me, small-stream fly-fishing means more than just fishing those little streams that are often chock-full of native and streambred trout. It reflects the total process of searching for, finding, and fishing these small streams, and catching, then promptly releasing, those worthy, wily fish.

But, you say, you've never even tried fishing one of those Lilliputian streams, let alone trying to delicately cast a fly into a narrow opening. You figure only a few bait fishermen fish these little brooks each season. Besides, many of these streams depend totally on a native population of trout. Few small streams receive any stocking of trout

1

from the states. As a result, if you were to fly-fish on the small streams you know, all you'd catch would be undersized native trout. Furthermore, these small streambred fish are extremely wary and spooky— one step near the stream, and you'll see them dart upstream or downstream under a bank.

Who wants to catch these little trout on a stream heavily enclosed with a canopy of brush and trees? Who wants to creep or crawl with his fly rod in search of small native trout? What type of fisherman would abandon larger waters for these small, heavily canopied streams?

Try fly-fishing on small streams before you condemn it. Small-stream fly-fishing becomes habit-forming. Once you experience a successful thirty-plus-trout day, you'll be hooked for life. Once you witness the uncluttered streams with beautiful native brook, cutthroat, rainbow, or streambred brown trout, you'll return again and again. And words like "solitude," "spectacular scenery," and "wilderness" immediately come to mind when I think of all those small streams I've fly-fished within the past ten years.

But before you go out to a small stream and try your luck, you've got to prepare properly. Don't expect to appear on a small stream and use the same equipment and techniques you've been using on that big river near your home. Don't expect to wade right next to that native trout rising above you. It's in preparing you for small streams that this book should come in handy. In the past couple of years, I have flyfished many small streams with the undisputed dean of fly-fishermen, George Harvey. Many of the tactics, techniques, and patterns, and a good deal of small-stream savvy that he taught me, are presented in the following chapters.

Much of the gear you've grown accustomed to on those large streams and rivers is of little use to you here. That nine-foot graphite you use with the ten-foot leader becomes worthless. You'll use one much shorter—just three fourths as long. And those waders you use to reach the rising trout on the last river you fished? Forget about them.

Casting techniques you finally feel comfortable with on large streams and rivers often won't work on diminutive streams. How many times did you check behind you when you fly-fished the expansive Madison or Henry's Fork? Remember, also, all that casting room you had from that drift boat on the McKenzie near Eugene, Oregon? Those are luxuries quickly forgotten on small streams. You now have little or no room to cast in front, to the back, or to the sides of you. Now it's time to innovate. Ralph Dougherty had a point when he said our subject was like fishing in a tunnel.

What about your habitually casual approach to many larger streams? Remember how close you could wade to that rising trout on the Madison River in Montana? Forget about that on these small streams. If you get too close, you'll see only a faint blur of an escaping trout darting underneath the far bank.

You won't find many instances in the present book where I mention specific small streams to fish. Many of these small streams can't take the pressure that their larger main stems can. As I remarked, small streams in most cases depend on native brook, streambred brown, native rainbow, or native cutthroat trout for their fish population. Few have any artificial stocking. Trout killed on these small streams take years to replace. Any mention of a specific small stream would send dozens of fly-fishermen overrunning that water.

What will you find in the book? The following chapters contain a lot of information on small-stream fly-fishing for trout. I've designed the material to acquaint you with much more than just tactics, techniques, and the equipment you'll need to make your stay on that small stream a pleasant one.

If small-stream fishing is so different from fishing larger streams, then there should be distinct advantages and disadvantages to this type of fly-fishing that you need to know about before you begin. Do you dislike fly-fishing on streams and rivers teeming with other fishermen? We'll introduce you to small streams by looking at advantages like privacy, dependable cold water, and many others. But we've already indicated that small streams have many liabilities, too. We'll look at advantages and disadvantages of small-stream fly-fishing in Chapter 1.

Where and how do you find these small streams? What are some of the prerequisites to look for in a small stream? In Chapter 3 you'll learn how to locate your own small streams by examining more than a dozen important criteria.

The problem with many newcomers to the small-stream routine is that they want to continue to fly-fish on small stocked streams. In the section of Chapter 2 titled "Getting Off the Beaten Track," I suggest ways to look for new waters and what you've got to do to experience successful small-stream fly-fishing.

How does your stream stack up to others in your area? How does it compare to those in other areas of the state, the region, and the nation? Another section in Chapter 2 recommends criteria you might use to compare the productivity of one small stream against another. It suggests ways you can omit some of the poorer streams and discover new, more worthwhile waters. It will help you rate the productivity of small streams.

There are good small-stream fly rods and poor ones. There are also appropriate and ill-suited leaders for these waters. Once you fly-fish these small streams, you'll see how important the correct fly rod, reel, and leader become. Chapter 3 provides you with information on fly rod and reel selection and some suggestions on leader makeup. It also includes information on other gear you'll need to take with you to make your stay an enjoyable one.

How do you roll cast? How do you use the bow-and-arrow cast? How do you approach the stream? Use the correct small-stream techniques, and you'll catch trout. Conversely, use poor tactics along even the most productive small streams, and you're in for a frustrating day. Chapter 4 suggests some effective techniques and tactics for small streams.

Small streams often run full in early spring and after a thunderstorm. Antithetically, in late summer many of these waters barely flow with a trickle. Different water levels require different fly-fishing methods, especially on small streams. Chapter 4 also studies what techniques and patterns work best with varying water levels.

Small streams are not without their hatches. Many small streams in the East contain downright spectacular Green Drake and Quill Gordon hatches. Other streams in the East, Midwest, and West hold various hatches of Tricos, Blue Quills, stoneflies, and caddis flies. Hit one of your favorite small streams when the Green Drake decides to appear, and all bets are off on rising trout. You'll see native trout lose their timidity and chase the emerging adults. Chapter 5 details some of the hatches you might encounter on small streams.

Fishing these small streams with dry flies requires that the pattern you use be extremely buoyant and easy to see. What about using nymphs, wet flies, and streamers? In Chapter 6 you'll learn more about patterns that have proved to be effective on these tributaries.

You'll also see suggested patterns and tying descriptions for some small-stream patterns in Chapter 7. Remember, it's important to carry high-floating dry flies with you to those small streams. Chapter 7 should help you tie appropriate flies that float well, that you can see, and that consistently catch trout on small streams.

Small streams are not without their problems. Posted land, acid rain, acid mine drainage, and creeping urbanization are only a few of the dilemmas confronting the future of small-stream fly-fishing. Chapter 8 looks at these and other problems that affect small streams.

You'll read about some philosophical questions in Chapter 9. Should you show others your favorite small streams? How much pressure can a small stream take and still be good? Should you keep any trout on these small streams?

Chapter 9 also examines other aspects of small-stream fly-fishing. How can you or your fishing group or organization make small-stream fly-fishing even better? Look at the proposals in Chapter 9 which you might want to incorporate on your favorite water to improve the small streams: adding lime to some of the more acid streams, designating no-kill areas, and baseline surveys. Many other avenues are also explored. This chapter looks, too, at such issues as joining an organization, policing violators, keeping waters open, and undertaking studies to improve water quality. These and other measures can guarantee the future of fishing on streams large and small.

In Chapter 10 we look at a small stream through the eyes of a legend in fly-fishing, George Harvey. I have had the pleasure of fly-fishing dozens of small streams with George and seeing him perform his fly-fishing magic on native trout. George has taught me more about small-stream fly-fishing than any other fisherman.

In Chapter 11 we take a parting glance at small-stream fly-fishing.

Enjoy reading the book. Continue to search diligently until you find that highly productive small stream that only you know exists. Then make that spectacular small stream your best-kept secret!

Advantages and Disadvantages of Small-Stream Fly-Fishing

BY AUGUST OF the record-hot summer of 1988, trout had abandoned many eastern and midwestern streams and rivers that had previously held them. Waters normally containing streambred trout, holdovers, and stocked fish lost them to warm water. Smallmouth bass inhabited many cold-water streams where trout had previously been found. Cool trout waters were at a premium.

About that time a friend of mine decided to take up fly-fishing for the first time. He begged me to take him out for his first trip to a stream. This novice chose August 5 to show up at my house and asked to go fly-fishing. Where could I take him on this 90-degree day? One of the tailwater fisheries less than two hundred miles away might do. These tailwaters empty cold water from or near the bottom of the impoundment above. Several local limestone streams like Big Fishing and Elk creeks held respectable cool temperatures. I opted, however, for a small local mountain stream only ten miles from my house. I knew this freestone stream had a good supply of streambred brown and native brook trout and temperatures rarely above 65 degrees.

When we arrived at the fast-flowing, boulder-strewn stream, I immediately checked the water temperature. This fine productive freestone stream hadn't let me down. The thermometer recorded 60 degrees on that hot afternoon. I was certain we'd experience a great day.

We didn't, however! Within a half-hour the fly-fisher who accompanied me asked to quit and moved to a larger stream. On almost every cast on this hemlock-lined, rhododendron-covered water, he got hung up in a bush. This beginner probably made no more than two or three good casts in the half-hour of fishing. That taught me an important lesson in small-stream fly-fishing: don't take a beginner to one of these streams with a heavy canopy and brush-lined banks. That's only one of the disadvantages of fly-fishing on small streams. There are plenty of others.

But small streams also have their advantages: the cool water we found in a hot summer is one of them. Let's look at some of the others in more detail.

Advantages of Small-Stream Fly-Fishing

I enjoy hiking into small streams. I like the uncluttered environment that these isolated areas present to the angler. I relish fly-fishing on some secluded creek that might not have seen another fisherman in a year or more. I enjoy fly-fishing for trout that don't much care what fly I present. In most cases, with a proper presentation, the native fish will take the fly. These fish don't have the luxury trout in larger streams have; they often won't carefully inspect each morsel floating over them. They eagerly take almost anything that looks like a free meal. This is the domain of the native trout.

I remarked earlier that several years ago the East and Midwest experienced the hottest summer on record. Many cities endured more than twenty days with temperatures over 90 degrees. Anglers saw fish kills on streams that had held trout for years. Water temperatures on the Au Sable in Michigan neared 70 degrees; on the Beaverkill, close to 80 degrees; and on Penns Creek, near 80. Where could one find any cold temperatures consistently? Tailwaters below dams with bottom releases and spring creeks still held cold water, and, of course, many small mountain streams still had temperatures in the sixties.

Ten years ago I met Al Gretz and Terry Carlsen at Canyon Village in Yellowstone Park. We headed toward Henry's Fork in eastern Idaho to fish the Western Green Drake. Terry waded into the expansive water and headed for the far bank. He stopped ten feet short and started casting toward the bank. He kept his back to 150 feet of water. Terry pretended Henry's Fork was only ten feet wide. He now felt confident. He pretended he was fly-fishing back East on one of his favorite haunts—a small stream.

Terry dislikes the large western rivers because he has difficulty reading them. Those heavy, deep rivers conceal boulders, rocks, and other cover that harbor trout. Small streams, on the other hand, disclose their trout more readily. Look at the far side of that small stream. See that undercut bank? Certainly a trout lives there. And that large boulder in the riffle at the head of the pool? There's probably another native fish near that.

Recently I met an old fly-fisherman on a small stream. We stopped and chatted for a while. I asked him why he didn't fish some of the larger streams and rivers nearby which contained some hefty rainbows and browns. He complained that at his advanced age he didn't trust himself wading heavy currents and big water. He felt completely at home wading these streams.

I asked Tucker Morris, of Spruce Creek, Pennsylvania, how he enjoyed fishing on Utah's Green River recently. Tucker indicated that he had returned home early from his trip because he couldn't contend with the powerful current found on that river. Tucker returned home to central Pennsylvania and some of his favorite small streams found there.

Many fly-fishermen don't feel comfortable on big streams and rivers with raging currents. Several years ago I fished on the Arkansas River near Buena Vista, Colorado. The Brown's Canyon area of the river was a raging torrent. After a few hours of fly-fishing on this dangerous river, I left it for a nearby small stream.

I've coached many young fly-fishermen in my lifetime. On most occasions I take them to a fairly large river to begin their attempt at fly-fishing. After these neophytes acquire some of the rudimentary casting skills necessary for presenting a fly, I then take them to smaller waters.

But big water can be difficult, too, for beginners. I've seen these anglers become frustrated when they couldn't reach trout rising to a hatch on big water. After several abbreviated, inadequate casts, they quit. Small-stream angling for relatively new fly-fishermen is much easier. Often they can sneak right up to the pool and gently cast a fly to the riffle above. No long casts with drag-free floats—just short casts that cover the water are required. Children especially appreciate the relatively forgiving aspects of small-stream fly-fishing where casting any distance is not really needed. Remember what I said earlier: start beginners off on a larger stream, then bring them to a smaller one after they've acquired the rudiments of casting.

What are some of the other benefits of fly-fishing on small streams in the middle of the summer? George Harvey and I recently fly-fished a small central-Pennsylvania stream. By the time we arrived at the rhododendron-choked stream, the sun had already warmed the air into the low eighties. The middle of July—no hatches—a hot summer sun shining through the heavy canopy time to fly-fish for trout—except when you're fly-fishing on small trout streams.

George and I hiked downstream two miles and planned to fish back upstream to the car. When we arrived at the stream, George complained how the canopy had grown over the water since he had last fished it ten years before. I wondered how we'd ever successfully fly-fish this small creek. Rhododendrons to the right and left of the stream, brush in the stream—all of it made a challenge even to the very best of fly-fishermen like George.

George and I decided to alternate fishing pools and productive pockets on our way back to the car. George fished the first fertile pool. On the second or third cast a heavy ten-inch streambred brown hit his size-14 ant. He moved up to the head of the same small pool and picked up a small brook trout.

We decided to keep count of the trout we caught that hot July day. In three hours of fly-fishing on that small, productive stream, George and I caught more than thirty native trout. How would we have done on a larger stream or river during the same time? In the three hours we fly-fished, we never saw another fisherman—not even a sign that fishermen had been in the area recently. All of this activity occurred on a small stream on a hot July afternoon. What more could you ask for?

George and I have hiked to many small streams. Many of these trips have occurred in June, July, and August in the middle of the day, a time when most of us prefer not to fly-fish. On each of these trips we kept a running count of the number of trout we caught. On good days we'd catch well over forty fish; on poor days, near twenty. Depending on the stream, about half of the fish measured more than six inches long.

Fish on one of hundreds of eastern or midwestern larger streams and

A typical small stream in Oregon. Oregon grape and salal crowd the banks.

rivers in April and May, and you'll catch trout. But hit these same waters in June, July, or August, and some will be barren. Look at Pine Creek in north-central Pennsylvania. Pine is your typical large free-stone stream that warms into the eighties in June. Fish the main stem of this watershed, and you'll likely experience a poor day. When the water warms on Pine, it quickly becomes a smallmouth bass haven.

However, if you fish one of the dozen or so cold-water tributaries of Pine Creek, you'll see plenty of trout. Some branches have thousands of stocked trout migrating up these cooler runs. You'll also find other fish in these headwater streams that have lived there all their lives. Many of these branches are small and have a meager flow in late summer, but they still hold a good number of streambred fish.

If you hit one of the thousands of small streams with some knowledge of what you're getting into, you're in for a pleasant surprise. If you realize some of the disadvantages to fly-fishing these types of miniature waters, you'll be prepared to adapt and accept these smaller environs.

You'll see small streams with few paths and no signs of recent fishermen, many of them brim-full of native trout waiting for any buggy-looking fly pattern. You'll often catch beautiful streambred trout on dry flies or wet flies when no hatch appears. Trout almost seem anxious to take any fly you present properly. You'll wade upstream cautiously in cool water that often holds trout year-round. And you'll often witness all of this in a background of scenic splendor which few other fly-fishermen experience.

Hatches appear infrequently on many small streams. Much of the time you're prospecting for trout rather than fishing over rising trout. But throw in an added bonus of a Green Drake or other insect hatch on one of these streams, and you'll think you've died and gone to heaven. When a hatch appears on a small stream, trout grab anything that looks like the natural.

Disadvantages of Small-Stream Fly-Fishing

Before you get completely enamored of the attributes of small streams, you should be aware of some of their frustrations—the disadvantages—especially for fly-fisherman.

Forty years ago, as a kid, I fished a small stream that held a reservoir three miles below. This reservoir supplied our town's drinking water. I fished that stream weekly throughout the spring and early summer with live bait. I'd stand behind a tree and float a worm on a catgut leader into a pool. No finesse here—almost each week I'd hook a wary brook trout or two over twelve inches long.

After a hiatus of twenty-five years, I returned to my childhood favorite, this time with flies. I hiked in about four miles on the same old trail I used as a kid. I kept thinking about the lengthy hike back to the car. I had to climb a steep mountain before I reached the car.

I found myself retrieving my fly from a bush on almost every backcast. False casting on this small creek was almost impossible. Not until I realized that I didn't have to backcast on every cast did I start placing the dry fly over trout.

While I fly-fished this small stream, I thought of the wide-open Madison River in Yellowstone Park and how much easier it was to fly-fish there. I almost never have to check behind me to see if I have enough casting room. I could wade within a couple of feet of the rising trout on the Madison without scaring them. Not so with small-stream fly-fishing.

Those wary trout on this small stream proved to be too much of a match for me and my dry fly that day. After I finished fishing each pool, I saw one or two trout scurry from the section I had just fished. I gave up disgusted and frustrated that I couldn't catch more than a handful of undersized native brook trout.

Recently when I fly-fished the Oreti and Eglinton rivers on the South Island of the New Zealand, I fished over trout rising to a hatch copied by a pattern the locals call "Dad's Favourite." Each time I matched the hatch on these two rivers, I ended the episode with a half-dozen browns and rainbows from twenty to thirty inches long and weighing from four to nine pounds. Just the day before, Mike Manfredo and I fly-fished several smaller streams and caught plenty of trout, but none of these trout on this smaller stream came near the size of those we caught on the Eglinton and Oreti. There's some truth to the old saying that you should fish large water for large trout. Don't expect to catch lunkers on your favorite small stream. You'll often have to be content catching five- and six-inch fish.

Fishing small streams requires a wary approach to avoid scattering the trout. You say you don't like to creep, crawl, or hide behind any available object near the stream? Then you won't like small-stream fly-fishing. Once you get addicted to this type of fishing and the tactics involved, however, you'll find that positioning yourself is part of the

Often you'll find a heavy canopy and scarce room to cast on small streams. On this small stream Terry Malloy has to crawl to a casting position.

grand picture. Often the only way to reach that rising native trout is to creep and crawl for several feet. If you present yourself in full view to the trout, you'll only see the hurried glimpse of a trout darting under nearby cover.

But that's not all. I hate snakes—especially rattlesnakes and copperheads. In addition, I've had a hearing defect since childhood, and I can't hear certain sounds, like those a rattler makes when it's coiled and ready to strike. Fly-fishing those small streams on hot July and August afternoons brings out the snakes. In an average year, I'll encounter three or four. Wear thick hip boots, watch where you're walking, and don't put your hands down until you scan the area. Respect poisonous snakes; stay your distance from them; but don't let them dictate whether or not you'll fly-fish your favorite stream.

The limited number of trout presents another liability of small-stream fly-fishing. In a large stream or river, anglers who kill a limit of trout probably won't have the deleterious effect that they would on a small stream with a limited number of trout. Besides, some of the larger waters receive fish during the year to replace those taken. One or two skilled fly-fishermen who kill their catch can decimate a small stream's population.

George Harvey and I experienced what could happen to a small stream when a persistent fly-fisherman kills fish. George and I had fly-fished a small branch of Young Woman's Creek in north-central Pennsylvania. For several weeks we enjoyed tremendous success every time we fished it. George and I averaged thirty to fifty trout each afternoon. Then one day we met another fly-fisherman on the same branch. The man lived only a few miles from the stream and fished it daily. He took trout home with him from every visit to the water. Two weeks after George and I met the angler, we fished the area again. Where we had previously caught thirty to fifty trout, George and I caught a meager ten fish in an entire afternoon. When it depends totally on a natural population, and other anglers keep some fish, a small stream takes a long time to replace its population.

Coping with the Disadvantages on Small Streams

Fly-fishing small streams successfully requires some new tactics and strategies if you're going to cope with the disadvantages I just mentioned. Those who frequent small streams know many of them already. First, you have to accept the fact that these are native, wily trout that dart under cover with any uncharacteristic movement on your part. Second, to cope with the restricted space, you must use equipment designed for small-stream fly-fishing. Get into the proper casting position for the pool by keeping a low profile; use a short leader on a seven-foot fly rod; and you're in for a day of exciting fly-fishing.

2.
Fishing
Productive
Water

PRODUCTIVE SMALL TROUT streams can be found throughout
the United States. In the Catskills and Adirondacks in New York
you'll find plenty of these miniature streams with respectable native
trout populations. Vermont, New Hampshire, and Maine have their
share of small streams with good native trout populations, too. In
western Virginia's Smoky Mountains you'll also find a wealth of
productive small trout streams. Decide on an area you'd like to fish,
then explore that region thoroughly.

Highly productive small streams often go unfished in the West. Travel
in western Montana along the Bitterroot Range, and you'll encounter
hundreds of small streams flowing off the snowcapped mountains.
Granted, these streams flow extremely high from May to July and are
marginal after that, but many of them contain a good supply of cutthroat trout up to a foot long.

After you've decided where you're going to fly-fish, buy topographic
maps of the area and search them for small wooded streams. Look for
sizable areas within state and national parks, state forests, and game
lands. Many of these lands contain countless small streams with good
populations of native trout and very few fishermen.

15

It was almost ten years ago that my son, Bryan, and I fly-fished some of the great waters of the Yellowstone area. We fished the obligatory waters of the Yellowstone and Madison rivers, the Firehole, Gibbons, and Henry's Fork. Around July 4 these waters sometimes seem to hold more anglers than trout.

Bryan and I finally had enough of the crowds and decided to search for more remote small streams with few or no anglers. On our way to Bozeman, Montana, we came across a mountain brook, still in the park, that intrigued us. In early July it still held a good flow of water. We stopped and decided to fly-fish this small branch. Bryan caught more than thirty cutthroat trout in a half-mile section on an attractor pattern, the Patriot. Every pool and productive run held two and three fish.

We fly-fished many famous waters on that three-week trip to Idaho and Montana. The success we experienced on that small remote stream turned out to be the most memorable event of the entire trip.

Identifying Productive Water

How can you find productive small streams? Answers to the following questions should assist you in locating your own productive small streams:

1. Can you get to the stream?

You've located some excellent small streams in Montana on topo maps, but there's no road for miles. Hiking is almost impossible. What good is the stream? Several streams in central Pennsylvania were destroyed for fishing a few years ago by a tornado that devastated a hundred-mile strip two miles wide. The tornado all but blocked off a couple of good small streams in the area. Access to two of these small streams was completely closed due to the tornado.

Mud Run in the Poconos of northeastern Pennsylvania displays just how difficult some streams are to reach. Recently Mike Marinelli and Jay Kapolka took me to a section of this small, productive stream. We hiked for two miles before we came to the valley that holds the stream. We then had to crawl for a half-mile downhill through an almost impenetrable patch of rhododendron until we reached Mud Run. Both sides of the stream had a half-mile swath of thick bushes, and the only way to get near the water was to literally crawl underneath them on our hands and knees. Once we got to the stream, we were confronted with huge boulders along the bank and waterfalls every few hundred feet. We fly-fished a hundred yards of this difficult stream before we crawled back out to our car.

2. Is the stream fishable?

You've finally reached the small stream you've wanted to fish for years. But once there, are you able to cast? There are several streams in my area that contain a good supply of brook and brown trout. These streams, however, are impossible to fly-fish. Many are clogged with rhododendrons, alders, and other low-growing brush along the entire length of the stream.

The same problem afflicts the part of central Pennsylvania mentioned earlier, where a tornado tossed and twisted trees along stream banks and made some sections of productive native trout streams inaccessible.

Cave Creek flows through part of a short piece of northeastern Nevada. This small, spring-fed stream flows through patches of impenetrable alder. In many spots it's impossible to cast any fly onto the three-foot-wide surface. Here's where dapping (lifting the fly up and down on the surface) comes in handy.

3. Does the stream closely parallel a road?

Picturesque Weikert Run flows through ten wooded miles of central Pennsylvania. The stream has an abundant water supply that barely rises into the sixties in July. You'll find seven miles of stream flowing through state forest land. But Wiker is heavily fished, and you'll find few trout in the stream. A good dirt road parallels the lower five miles of Weikert and encourages many to fish the area. If you plan to fly-fish a small stream that follows a road, then search for a tributary to that stream or look for a section that leaves the road.

Look at Big Fill in central Pennsylvania as a good example. PA 350 closely parallels the lower three miles of the stream. Above that, the stream leaves the road. Recently I left George Harvey off on the section near the highway while I walked upstream away from the road. The farther I walked away from the road, the better the fishing became. I soon headed downstream and told George about the great fly-fishing upstream. He complained about the "lousy fishing" along the road. Try two or three areas of a stream before you exclude it from your list of high-quality small streams.

4. Does the state stock the section you're fishing?

Stocked streams invite hordes of anglers to their shores. Many states even stock small, inconspicuous streams. When they do, they harm the native trout populations found in these waters. We just discussed Weikert Run. The state stocks this small stream preseason and at least one time in-season. This and many more small streams can't take the fishing pressure placed on them by this artificial influx of trout. In the end it severely hurts the native population of the stream.

5. Does the stream contain decent pools and riffles?

The definitive work on stream diversity and productivity is *Trout Streams*, by Paul Needham (Winchester Press, New York, 1969). In his discussion of productive waters Needham suggests that long shallow riffles hold few trout. He indicates that the best makeup for a productive stream is one that contains 50 percent riffles and 50 percent pools. He says that riffles hold the food (nymphs), while pools afford the necessary shelter for the fish. "Both are essential and, properly arranged, form the ideal fishing stream."

This productive pool netted five cutthroat and rainbow trout.

There's a small stream near my home that might be Needham's ideal stream. It falls considerably in a short distance and forms deep pools with equal numbers of riffles between. You don't have to walk more than a few feet from one pool or pocket to another—all teeming with brook and brown trout. This type of small stream is the exception rather than the rule, however.

Some of the small western streams fall precipitously from high mountain ranges. Many of these contain numerous small pools teeming with cutthroats.

Then there are other streams which contain few productive pools and riffles. Often you have to hike a couple of hundred feet from one productive section to another. You'll encounter many of these. Remember Needham's suggestion that the best streams are those with good riffles to hold the food and pools to hide the trout.

6. Does the stream contain good cover?
I'll never forget the time the Brodhead Chapter of Trout Unlimited invited me to watch an experiment they conducted. The chapter examined two contiguous sections of a small stream, Martin's Creek, located in eastern Pennsylvania. On the lower half of the study area, the chapter made many improvements, adding rocks and boulders and building downstream Vs, dams, and other devices that improved the habitat and cover for trout. On the upper half, the control section, the chapter did nothing. Two years previously, when the state electroshocked the two sections, they found equal numbers of trout (eight) in the lower and upper halves.

Two years after the chapter made the improvements to the lower half, they invited me back to witness the results of a new fish census by the state. In the upper half of the experimental section, where the organization constructed no improvements, they again found eight trout. In the lower section, where the chapter had assiduously added improvements, the state now found thirty-six trout. What a great achievement—a fourfold increase in the number of trout a section of stream holds.

Each small stream develops its own personality. Some streams contain extensive deep pools peppered with large rocks and boulders. Does your favorite stream hold plenty of cover for trout? Are there huge boulders, brush, submerged trees, undermined banks to hide trout from predators?

Have you thought of adding some obstacles to the stream? By just making a few improvements, you can probably bring your favorite small stream to hold more and larger trout. I have a couple of pet small streams locally. Each time I fish them, I add a couple of big boulders here, a few rocks there, some brush at another place. Over the years, I'm certain these meager improvements have increased the quantity of trout in that section. Before you do any such improvement, however, check with the landowner to make certain it's permissible. If it is, you'll be doing yourself and others a favor by adding a few improvements.

Recently George Harvey and I fished a small stream which seemed to hold few trout. In late September the pools held little water, and the riffles and pockets seemed void of trout. The ravine in which this stream flowed never widened to more than thirty feet. The steep mountains on either side of the stream scarcely allowed any sunlight to shine on any part of the stream. Rarely did the water on this stream rise above 60 degrees. What a great place for some damming devices and boulders placed strategically throughout! Each time I fish this stream, I spend a half-hour or more damming up several pools.

7. Is there a good food supply for the trout?
Turn over some rocks on the stream. Look for evidence of a good number of mayflies, caddis flies, and stoneflies. Are a couple of species of mayflies found on the stream? Does the stream contain some large mayflies like the March Brown, the Western March Brown, or the Green Drake? You'd be surprised how many small streams hold good hatches of these and other aquatic insects.

When you catch native trout on a stream, examine them. Are the heads unusually large for the size of the fish? Abnormal growth usually indicates that the trout in the stream mature slowly because of a shortage of food. Check the growth of trout on one small stream against another. You'll see variations.

8. Is there a good supply of two- to four-inch trout?
On several streams I've fished, I've found plenty of native trout over six inches long, but few smaller. To me that often suggests that conditions didn't warrant a good breeding season the past year or two.

George Harvey and I fly-fished a productive Pennsylvania stream a couple of years ago and caught a good supply of brook and brown trout from three to twelve inches long. After fishing a half-mile upstream, we caught no more trout. We fished a half-mile of barren water before we left the stream. George and I deduced that the upper section of the stream had evidently dried up the previous summer during an extensive drought. Watch for these telltale signs.

9. How do water level and temperature hold up during the summer?

The previous example of the section of stream barren of trout demonstrates the problem. If you've fly-fished a section of a small stream without success, you might question the pressure on the stream, the water temperature, or the water flow. Almost immediately upon entering a stream, I check the water temperature. If the temperature is near 70 degrees on a hot summer day, I look for cooler water. Even on hot summer afternoons many of these small streams should have temperatures below 65 degrees. Temperatures above 70 degrees put stress on trout, especially brook and cutthroat. In *Trout Streams* Needham says that the limiting temperature for brook trout is 75 degrees; for brown trout it's 81; and for rainbow trout, 83 degrees. Water temperatures above those listed may be fatal to trout.

Water levels can be deceiving, especially on western streams. Look at a small stream bank-full from snowmelt in June. Check that same stream in late August or September, and it might be completely dry. If you plan to fly-fish any small stream, make certain you check the water flow in late summer.

10. What kinds of trout does the stream contain?

I prefer fly-fishing over streambred brown or rainbow trout because they're more wary and often grow larger than the native brook trout. That's sacrilegious to many old-time small-stream enthusiasts who prefer fly-fishing over native brookies. Many streams in the East and Midwest have mixed populations of brook and brown trout. A few have mixed populations of streambred rainbow and native brook trout.

Within the past couple of decades brown trout have invaded and inhabited many of the waters earlier earmarked for brook trout. Many small waters now hold brown trout in their lower sections, a mixture of brown and brook in the middle section, and brook trout only in the very upper reaches of the stream.

Many of the small streams in the West have cutthroat populations

Using a thermometer.

in their upper ends and rainbow, brown, and cutthroat downstream. Look at the Bitterroot River in Montana. In the main stem, near Hamilton, the Bitterroot contains some brown, rainbow, and a few cutthroat trout. Many of the tributaries flowing from the range to the West contain only cutthroat trout.

11. Is the stream heavily fished?

George Harvey looks for fishing pressure on a small stream even before we begin to fish. What does he look for? He'll search for small bits of paper like candy wrappers, cigarette packs, or cigarette butts scattered near the stream. He looks at the grass near the water to see if any fishermen have carved a recent path. He examines the banks on both sides of the stream for an angler's path. If George notes a lack of fish, few strikes, and a well-worn path near the stream, he looks for a more remote area on the stream he's fly-fishing, or he moves on to another stream.

Not long ago George and I fly-fished a small stream for an hour without much success. Along the stream we found part of the contents of a discarded sandwich. When we looked more closely, we saw fresh boot tracks next to the stream. We moved away from that section of the small stream to a more remote area just a few miles away and began catching native brook trout up to ten inches long.

The number of cabins and camps along a branch or tributary can give you a clue to fishing pressure. George and I fly-fished a productive small tributary in late April and again in July. We caught more than thirty brook and brown trout on that stream early in the year. When we returned in July, we caught very few trout and saw many signs of fishing pressure along the stream. We hiked up the stream several miles and saw a camp that had two cars parked out front. No wonder we didn't catch many trout! This group at the camp had been dining on native trout all week long.

12. Does the stream have any productive tributaries or branches?

Sometimes a small stream can be heavily fished while anglers overlook one of its productive branches. That's why it's important to carry topographic maps with you on any of your excursions. Don't worry about the size of the water. Some very small branches and tributaries can hold large trout. Trout stocked in marginal streams will

Ken Helfrich of Springfield, Oregon, releases a heavy cutthroat from a productive tributary of central Oregon's McKenzie River.

often seek out small cold branches for the remainder of the hot summer.

Here's an instance where large stocked trout will inhabit small cold streams. Pine Creek in north-central Pennsylvania holds a good supply of trout throughout much of the season. When June arrives and Pine warms above 80 degrees, trout move out of the main stem into any cool water available. This cold water might be Slate Run, Cedar Run, or a dozen other small streams that flow into the main stem. On occasion I wait until Pine warms, then I head up one of the cool tributaries. If you hit one of these branches after a heavy downpour, you'll often catch trout just moving up to the colder water. The influx of additional water makes the journey upstream much easier for the trout. In some of the pools near Pine these tributaries hold hundreds of trout migrating upstream to reach colder water.

13. Is the pH of the stream above 6.0?
It's also important to consider whether the small stream you plan to

fly-fish has been affected by acid rain. Many of the streams in the Northeast receive rainfall with a highly acid pH of 4-5 (neutral is 7). Acid rain has eliminated trout from some of our once-productive streams. Continually check the pH of small streams with a pH-tester. The acidity of a stream severely affects the quantity and quality of the trout population and the diversity and number of aquatic insects in the stream.

Thirty years ago none of us would have considered checking the pH of small streams. With the recent knowledge about acid rain, it's important to know how well the small streams you fly-fish are holding up. Many small eastern streams have lost their native trout populations because of high acidity. The experiment on Linn Run in southwestern Pennsylvania and the effects a pH lower than 5 had on that stream point out dramatically why pH is an important consideration. You'll find information on the experiments on Linn Run in southwestern Pennsylvania in Chapter 8.

Locating Small Streams

It's part of the total small-stream experience to constantly search for new streams to fly-fish. Decide on the general area you would like to explore; then buy topographic maps of that area. The up-to-date statewide DeLorme atlases now available for Maine, New Hampshire, Vermont, New York, Pennsylvania, Ohio, Michigan, Illinois, Minnesota, Wisconsin, Tennessee, Virginia, Florida, Washington, Oregon, Northern California, and Southern & Central California are also an excellent resource (DeLorme Mapping, Freeport, Maine, 1990).

Topographic maps can tell you a lot about a small stream even before you see it. Learn to use them properly to decide whether or not a small stream warrants a closer look. Does the stream flow through a wooded area? Does it drop rapidly? Are there any tributaries? Does a road closely parallel the stream? Does a trail, power, or gas line cross or parallel the stream? Does the stream flow through public land? Are there any abandoned strip mines nearby? All of these and many other questions can be answered by studying topographic maps carefully.

Many of the larger colleges, universities, and municipal libraries have topographic maps of their areas. You can also purchase maps from the federal government. (Chapter 3 tells you where you can order these maps.) If you plan to fly-fish small streams seriously, then spend some time gleaning important information from topographic maps.

Many states provide maps of their streams and rivers. The Nevada Department of Wildlife furnishes a map showing their three grades or classes of streams. For each grade they assign a different color. Grade 1 streams host numerous native trout; Grade 2, a few; and Grade 3, none. For other states, like Montana, Colorado, and Pennsylvania, you'll find books written about the streams of the state. Each is a valuable tool, and each lists some of the smaller streams in the state that carry good numbers of trout.

Additionally, each state has national and state forest maps which list many small streams. New York has an excellent map that shows all the tributaries of the Beaverkill. Many of these carry their own native brook and brown trout populations. Recently the Pennsylvania Fish Commission conducted a survey to ascertain what streams in the state carried good native-trout populations. This list, by county, contains nearly a hundred productive wild-trout fisheries.

Let's look at a sample map of a typical area that contains some good small streams. You'll see state game lands and state forest lands on the map. Four different runs flow out of these public lands. Look for the following on the map:

1. Roads.
2. Trails.
3. Branches or tributaries to the streams.
4. How much does Bear Run drop in its first mile?
5. Does Brush Creek flow through forest or field?
6. Why is the date of the map survey important?
7. Does Pine Creek flow all year?
8. How many named branches does Brush Creek have?
9. Which stream has a road paralleling its entire length?
10. Which stream is farthest from a road?

Before you decide to fish an area, you might want to check out the local streams with someone. Talk to a park ranger or warden or a hunter who has traveled up and down the stream. All can be helpful and may know a lot about local small streams. If possible, talk to a fisherman who has fished the stream; but, remember, on most occasions, local anglers guard their hidden small streams. Why should they share them with any stranger?

Once you reach your destination, it shouldn't take you long to see

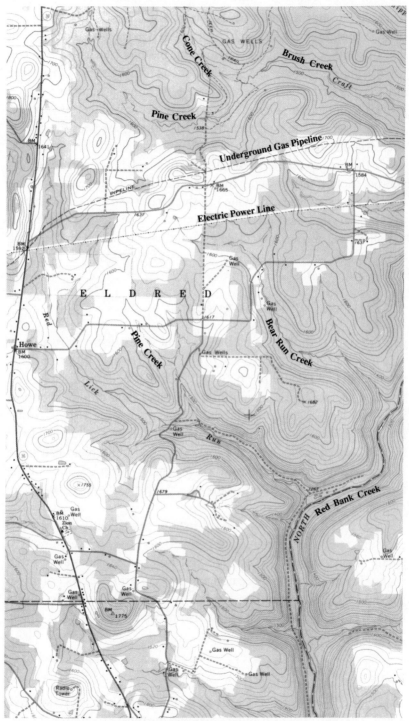

Studying a topographic map beforehand can tell you a great deal about the terrain and make small stream exploring much easier and more productive.

if the stream has a good population of trout. First check the water temperature. Is it well below 70 degrees? If you carry a pH-tester with you, check the acidity of the stream. Is the pH above 6? Above 7? Then lift up a couple of rocks and stones to check for insect life. Do you see any mayfly nymphs, any caddis larvae, or stonefly nymphs?

Look along the stream bank for signs of recent fishing pressure. Do you see a worn path near the stream? Has the grass near the stream been recently trod on?

Try fly-fishing on the stream for a half-hour. If you strike out, try another section farther away from the road or trail. Remember to use the rating system discussed later in this chapter so you can compare the stream with other more familiar streams you've fly-fished.

You'll be surprised how these expeditions pay off in future fishing fun.

What Types of Water to Fish

George Harvey dropped me off next to the creek. I slowly fished my way upstream a half-mile to where he planned to park the car. Pocket after pocket and pool after pool looked like it held trout. None did. Only occasionally did I pick up a trout and then only in the most unlikely places. Deep pools on this small stream didn't yield a trout. Productive-looking pocket water yielded few fish. I concluded from this and several other similar experiences that this stream had some fishing pressure. If I happened to cast the fly over sections of the stream that hadn't been hit in the past couple of days, I'd catch an occasional trout.

If you feel the stream you're fly-fishing has recently experienced pressure, then fish those areas you think others have missed. Look for small, inconspicuous pockets and small holes next to trees and behind rocks. Try some of the more noticeable pools and pockets only with a couple of casts and move on. On small streams that have experienced recent pressure, concentrate your fishing on areas you think others have avoided.

Pools

This type of water presents a mystery. Pools are the least productive areas of a small stream at some times and the most productive at other times. If the small stream gets a great deal of fishing pressure, generally the most pressure occurs in the pools. I can tell by fly-fishing the pools just how much pressure a particular small stream gets. If you rarely catch a trout in these pools, then the stream gets pressure. If, on the other hand, you catch one or more trout in almost every pool, then you can surmise that pressure on the stream is insignificant.

On occasions I've met my match with a pool on a small stream. More times than I'd like to recall, I've bypassed pools because there was no way of properly fly-fishing them. Look at a typical pool lined on both sides with a thick brush border. Rhododendrons totally block off the upper end, both the right and left banks, and the tail. On those stretches I just bypass the section and move upstream.

Fly-fishing pools on small streams presents several distinct disadvantages. Trout see the leader more easily and have more time to study the pattern than they do in faster water. Trout often refuse to come from the bottom of a deep pool to take a dry fly on the surface.

Don't overlook the tail of the pool. I forget the number of times I have paraded clumsily into the tail section to fish the pool above and moved one or two heavy trout. These trout, in turn, alerted the trout up at the head of the pool.

Remember what Needham says in his book *Trout Streams:* trout need some deep pools in which to hide.

Riffles

Most small streams alternate deep and shallow areas. The deep areas constitute the pools and the shallow areas the riffles. H.B.N. Hynes in *The Ecology of Running Waters* (University of Toronto Press, 1972) states that riffles are spaced equidistant from five to seven stream widths apart in many streams.

The majority of the aquatic insects in a stream inhabit the riffles. However, many riffles on small streams are too shallow to hide trout. Fish do move into these areas to feed, especially when a hatch appears, but after they feed in the riffles, they move back to deeper or protected water.

Pockets

Pockets are those deep little sections behind and around rocks and boulders. These are difficult for a bait fishermen to fish properly and therefore are productive areas even on streams that get fishing pressure. Some small streams contain few, if any, of these pockets between pools; others contain many. The boulders you'll find in pockets give trout the protection they need from predators.

Fish both above and below the rocks in pocket areas. You'll also find trout lying in drift lines along the edges of rocks waiting for terrestrials and aquatic insects.

Deep water under trees and brush

Notice that tree or branch on the far side. Does a trout live under that cover? How many times have I answered that question with a resounding strike under a bush, branch, or other obstruction in a small stream? Don't overlook any of these snags when fly-fishing these waters. Especially under low water conditions, trout need cover to hide from predators.

Undercut banks

Many of the small streams I fly-fish have undercut sections that run for a couple of feet under a bank. I always attempt a float or two within inches of the bank and let the fly drift the entire distance along the undercut section. Many times trout come out from their concealed positions under the bank to take an artificial. Never overlook these potential hiding places for lunker trout; they protect trout from the ravages of predation and are the single most important hiding area for native trout.

Above a dam

George Harvey had heard reports that one of his favorite small streams harbored huge brown trout in October. These trout left their normal home in the lake below to move upstream for their fall migration and egg-laying. Trout well over twenty inches long make the journey annually.

Pennsylvania's fish laws prohibit anglers from harvesting fish on wild-trout waters after Labor Day, however. This policy prohibits anglers from killing any of the wild-water breeders that move upstream in fall. If the laws were different, many heavy breeders would be killed just upstream from an impoundment. If your state does allow fly-fishing on small streams when trout migrate for breeding, then you can expect to see some monsters moving up the small streams.

Beaver dams

Recently created beaver dams often hold some large native trout. Many of these dams are ten to fifteen feet deep with plenty of cover for trout. But after a couple of years, the water in many dams grows warmer and the pH lower, and pan fish and pickerel replace the earlier trout population. Downstream from these dams the water often runs too warm for trout until cooler tributaries or branches enter the main stem.

New beaver dams often create unusual casting problems. Often alders and other low-lying bushes line the banks of these dams, preventing any accurate casting. If the dam is fairly large and some areas not too deep to wade, you might work your way stealthily to some rising fish.

Many years ago I came upon a large beaver dam formed in an open area of a small mountain stream. When I appeared at the breast of twigs and branches, I saw a dozen brook trout rising in the impoundment. For more than two years I'm certain I was the only angler who fished this dam. For those years this was my domain.

Rating Your Favorite Small Streams

What a beautiful small mountain trout stream I fly-fished today! This picturesque stream contained plenty of pools, pockets, and undercut banks to hold native trout. For more than thirty years I had fly-fished this same small creek. Now, after more than ten years away from the stream, I was back, anxious to fly-fish this productive water again. I can remember thirty years ago when I first fished this water; it wasn't unusual to catch forty, fifty, or more native trout in a half-day's fishing. Many of these fish averaged eight to ten inches long with an occasional trout over a foot long.

But not any more. This day that I reappeared on one of my favorite streams netted me a meager half-dozen four- to six-inch fish in four hours of fishing.

What had happened to one of my favorite streams to reduce the trout

Andrew Leitzinger consistently rates this small eastern stream at the top of his list.

population so dramatically? Several factors combine to produce the decline of many of our once-productive small streams. Acid rain, overfishing, predation, low water, and pollution all take a toll on these once-productive small streams.

Where do I now find above-average small-stream fly-fishing? What streams still contain a good supply of native fish? If you start to keep a chart of the small streams you fish and use several criteria to rate them, you'll ensure yourself a good backlog of productive small streams. That way you won't put too much pressure on any stream. When you fish a stream that doesn't compare favorably with its productivity several years back, don't cross it off the first time. If, however, it fails to produce on two or three occasions, pass over the stream for several years. If the stream still hasn't come back after a respite of several years, cross it off your list.

It's easy to keep records and rate your own favorite small streams. Use a system that's acceptable to you, but start doing it immediately. You'll be surprised how many times you'll refer back to your data. You can simply list the trout you catch per hour, or you can make the rating system more elaborate. Construct one that fits your needs and abilities. Following are some of the items you might want to make a part of your rating scale:

1. Number of trout caught per hour of fishing; or strikes per hour of fishing.
2. Size of the trout caught (optional).
3. Number of hatches on the stream (optional).
4. Fishing pressure (subjective).
5. Rating of the pools, pockets, and cover (subjective).

Let's look at each of the guidelines:

1. Number of trout caught or number of strikes per hour

Why did you plan to fish the stream in the first place? Sure, you might enjoy the scenery and solitude that a small, isolated stream offers. You also might enjoy fishing the pools and riffles on the stream. But no matter how much you enjoy that, you've traveled to this particular stream to catch trout on a fly. The number of trout is therefore the most significant criterion you can use in rating the stream. Keep a mental record of the number of fish you catch per hour on the stream you're fishing. If you fish the water from 2:00-3:30 PM and catch fifteen trout, then you averaged ten trout per hour on that trip (see Stream B in Table 1).

You might want to use number of strikes per hour if you feel more comfortable with that. Grouse hunters use number of flushes per hour as an indicator of the density of grouse in an area. This might be especially important if you're just a beginner at fly-fishing.

Check the stream several times a year to get a more accurate number of fish the stream contains. You might experience a bad day, on occasion, even on a good stream so it's imperative that you check the stream several times before excluding it. Also, check several different areas on the stream.

2. Size of the trout caught

On several small creeks I've fly-fished the past couple of years, I've caught dozens of trout. All of these native trout averaged three or four inches long. Very seldom did I ever catch any trout on those streams over six inches long. I prefer catching larger trout, so a criterion that includes size is an important part of an overall rating system in small-stream fly-fishing for me. Count the number of trout over seven inches long that you average per hour on the small stream you're fishing.

Of course, if someone recently fished the section of the stream you're rating, your numbers will be skewed. Again, it's important to check a stream several times before you give up on it. I indicated above that this criterion is quite subjective. If you don't feel comfortable with it, discard it.

3. Hatches

On many of the small streams you fly-fish you won't know what hatches are to be expected. If you have difficulty with this criterion, omit it. You're simply comparing one small stream you know against another. If you rate the small stream a 5, then that stream contains a good number of insect hatches. A rating of 4 means the stream contains fewer hatches, down to 1, which indicates the stream contains very few insects.

Why are the number of hatches a stream possesses important? Each significant hatch on a small stream is a special event. It provides a bonus feeding spree for the native fish. Just fly-fish a small stream when the Green Drake appears. You'll see the small stream come alive with feeding, voracious trout that have suddenly lost their timidity. These once-wary trout become easy to catch when a hatch appears.

Conversely, look at another small stream nearby that contains no Green Drake hatch. Here you continuously have to prospect for trout. The hatch makes all the difference. George Harvey relates how he fished on a small stream recently and saw Green Drakes emerging all afternoon. George just walked from pool to pool searching for trout rising to the drakes. He picked up dozens of fish—one brown trout measured nineteen inches long.

If you know the hatches on most of the small streams you fly-fish, then use this criterion. If you have difficulty comparing the number of hatches on this stream with others, then skip it. There are other clues to food supply besides hatches. As we saw earlier, often on small streams you'll catch small-bodied native trout with large heads. This usually suggests a poor food supply. If you start catching a lot of these unusual trout, you'd better check the stream for insect life.

The number of hatches refers to the number or estimate of different species for the entire year.

4. Fishing pressure

George Harvey and I recently met a fly-fisherman on the Left Branch of Young Woman's Creek. George stopped and talked with him for a while. The angler fished the branch three or four times a week and killed his catch each time. The past week or so, the local had caught and killed eight trout each day. He was the only angler George and I had encountered on the stream for several weeks. Would this mean the stream had fishing pressure? Yes! Assigning a number to an item like fishing pressure is again subjective. Rate your streams from 1 to 5, with those having little or no pressure a 5 and those under heavy fishing pressure a 1.

5. Deep holes and pockets, and cover

Paul Needham, in *Trout Streams*, suggests that long, flat, shallow riffles hold few trout because of a lack of shelter and that deep pools interspersed with frequent riffles make the best type of cover. Needham says that the riffles produce most of the food, and the pools contain shelter for the trout. Look for this critical mix of pools and riffles when you rate the makeup of a small stream.

There are several streams—since crossed off my list—that contain few pockets and pools. Pockets, pools, undercut banks, boulders, and other deeper water and obstructions hide trout from predators and other fishermen. The better the stream in terms of cover, the more trout it should hold—all other things being equal. Here again this rating character is subjective. Rate the small streams you fish from 1 to 5. Those rated a 5 are the best, with a 1 the poorest.

Let's look at a sample of some of the small streams I've fished and see how the simple rating system works.

Table 1: Rating a Stream

Stream	A	B	C	D	E
Trout/hour	15	10	7	5	5
Number over 7 inches	10	5	4	2	1
Number of hatches	5	4	5	2	0
Fishing pressure	4	2	2	3	2
Deep pools	4	4	4	3	2
Totals	38	25	22	15	10

These figures are taken from actual fishing trips on small streams. I've devised an overall rating system like the following, based on the totals for each rated criterion:

1. 30 or higher: rated Number 1, or excellent fly-fishing.
2. 20-30: rated Number 2, or good fly-fishing.
3. 10-20: rated Number 3, or mediocre fly-fishing.
4. Below 10: rated Number 4, or poor fly-fishing.

Under my rating system in Table 1, only Stream A qualifies as a top-rated stream. Streams B and C rate as Number 2, and D and E classify as mediocre trout waters.

I indicated earlier that criteria such as fishing pressure and number of hatches are very subjective. You'll know the hatches on a stream only after you've fly-fished it for a long while. Even then you might have difficulty assigning a rating.

Some of the criteria might be difficult to obtain. Other criteria might be tough to estimate with any degree of reliability. How do you determine the fishing pressure on a small stream accurately? How do you rate the pools, pockets, and cover on a small stream? We already said that predicting the number of hatches on a small stream requires a familiarity with the water.

Here are some additional hints for your rating system:
1. Keep your rating list in a small note pad in your vest. Complete the rating immediately after you've finished fishing a small stream.
2. Try to hit each stream two or three times a year so you have a more accurate rating. Try to fish in low and high water and in spring and summer so you have a better feeling for the stream.
3. Keep crossing off poorer streams and looking for new, better ones. If small streams you continue to fly-fish consistently rate poorly, cross them off and hunt for new ones. Part of the fun of small-stream fly-fishing is the continuous process of discovering new waters. (Other chapters in the book recommend methods for finding new streams.)
4. Check results with a friend who has also fly-fished a certain stream and see how your rating compares with his.
5. Decide on a rating scale for your area. Move the rating numbers lower or higher for different areas of the United States. In some remote areas of Colorado and Montana, I've caught twenty and even thirty trout per hour. Under these circumstances an "excellent" small stream might rate forty and above. Conversely, if you live close to a metropolitan area, you might have to lower your scale.
6. The size of the fish caught might be distorted if the small stream you're fly-fishing contains a good supply of streambred brown trout.

These trout tend to inhabit the lower ends of small streams and leave the upper ends to brook or cutthroat trout. Brown trout grow larger than brook trout and will definitely alter your results.

7. Use a rating scale that fits the type of water you fish. If you omit hatches, you might want to rate a top stream from 25 and higher. If you include only number and size of trout, you might use 15 for a top rating.

8. Check the water temperature and pH of the small stream you plan to fish. If the water temperature seems to rise each year you fish the stream, you might question why. You might also consider looking for other, colder, small streams nearby.

   Acidity, measured by pH, strongly determines the health of small streams. If the pH has declined over the years, so will the hatches you see in the stream. It's important to record the pH of a stream every time you fish it.

9. Keep records. What's the sense of rating streams if you don't keep permanent records that you can refer to from time to time? Include the caddis fly, stonefly, and mayfly hatches you experience. You might want to refer to these. Later in the chapter you'll see a sample of a record-keeping system you can use.

With all the cautions of a rating system in mind, it's still a useful tool to evaluate small streams. Once you've had a chance to rate some of your streams, you can keep a list of your top small streams and share them with guests. I say guests, but not other local anglers—otherwise your pride and joy will soon be shared by a myriad of others and will no longer be a top-rated small stream.

Keeping Records

Since 1964 I've kept a record of every fishing trip I've made. I often refer back to these trips and the streams I've fished to check what hatches I saw, what type of trout I caught, what water temperatures I recorded, and what patterns and sizes caught the most trout. Each winter I look back over these records and reminisce about the good and bad fishing trips I've had over the years.

There's one measurement that I did not include in my records that I wish I had kept—pH. With a record of pH over the thirty years I've fly-fished, I'd have a fairly good idea how the small streams I've fished have held up to the onslaught of acid rain. I'd also have a better idea as to the correlation between trout populations and the pH of a stream. George Harvey and I surmise that one of the more important reasons for the decline in trout populations on small streams is the acid-rain phenomenon. I've since added pH as an important aspect of keeping records.

Following are some of the headings I use in my record book: Date, Stream, Location, Time of Day, Number of Trout, Size, Pattern and Size, Insects Seen, Numbers, Water and Air Temperature, pH, Rating.

I attempt to be as specific as I can on the location column, that being especially important if you want to check a hatch; insects can occur in one location and be absent a few feet away. Also one part of a stream can be much more productive than another.

Always record water and air temperatures. By comparing both you have a good idea how well your stream holds up to hot summer days over a long period.

If you record the number of trout caught, the size, and the hours fished, you'll already have enough information to compare one stream to another. Make certain, though, that you don't compare apples to bananas. If you fly-fish Stream A on a hot afternoon, don't compare the results on that stream to fly-fishing Stream B in the evening when a heavy Green Drake appears.

Note that in my record book I list a column that refers to the numbers of insects I see on a stream. I usually list this as tens, hundreds, or thousands to indicate the intensity of the hatch. Insects appearing in tens, of course, would make up a sparse hatch, while a count in hundreds or thousands would suggest a rather concentrated emergence.

The last column allows you to assign a number to your rating system. Remember, in our sample rating earlier we used 0 to 30 and above. Assign your own rating numbers.

Getting Off the Beaten Track

I know many fly-fishermen who enjoy fly-fishing only when they can see other anglers around them. Look sometime at the crowds fishing the Yellowstone and Madison rivers in Yellowstone Park. In a short stretch of water, you'll see dozens of fly-fishermen. Try fly-fishing Henry's Fork during a Western Green Drake hatch in late June and see how many other anglers are nearby. Witness the hordes of anglers on the Beaverkill in the Catskills of New York in April, May, and June. Scarcely a pool on any of these hallowed rivers and streams remains silent during the fishing season. Fish Penns Creek in central Pennsylvania during the Green Drake in late May and early June, and you'll see hundreds and hundreds of anglers strategically positioned along the banks awaiting the evening hatch.

Are you like so many of the fishermen who frequent the places I just mentioned? Do you fly-fish only on well-traveled roads? Do you have to fish in sight of other fishermen? Do you like to fly-fish in well-stocked streams and rivers? Then fly-fishing on small streams is not for you. You'll miss those thousands of miles of productive water that you have to hike to. You'll not enjoy those quiet, pristine waters.

Do you want to try small-stream fly-fishing? You'll have to forsake large streams and rivers, crowds of anglers, stocked trout, and a noisy environment and trade them for the peace, solitude, and beauty of a small mountain stream with no other anglers near you. You'll have to exchange that occasional large trout for many smaller native or streambred trout.

Vince Gigliotti and Al Gretz, of Punxsutawney, Pennsylvania, and I recently spent a day on some small streams in the Bob Marshall Wilderness Area just outside Glacier National Park in Montana. We had fly-fished on the large Flathead River without much success for several days. At every access to the river above Kalispell we saw anglers. We saw dozens of anglers.

Finally all three of us longed for a more isolated stream. We headed up the South Fork of the Flathead. We traveled fifty-five miles on dirt roads, saw several interesting small mountain streams, and finally decided to fly-fish one that flowed into a pristine lake. The stream ranged no wider than twenty feet across and at most places was less than fifteen. All three of us started in the lake because a hatch appeared when we arrived and trout rose all over the impoundment. We caught grayling and rainbows for several hours before the excitement abated.

I headed up the small stream for a few hundred feet while Vince and Al fished the lake. Vince cautioned me about wandering too far up the river in this wilderness. There had recently been reports about a grizzly bear in this same vicinity. Even on this cursory trip up the stream a few feet, I caught trout on this relatively unfished small stream.

When my son, Bryan, and I fly-fished in Yellowstone Park, even the

Tom Walsh releases a heavy brook trout from a small eastern stream.

smaller waters in the park, like the Firehole and Gibbons rivers, held too many anglers for us. We decided to head to a smaller stream and try our luck. Bryan was only twelve, and I watched and coached on this small stream as he fished. In pool after pool and pocket after pocket, Bryan picked up rainbow trout in this fifteen-foot-wide stream on the western side of the park. Many of the trout in this small stream measured more than twelve inches long. We quit two hours and forty-five trout later. Within twenty miles of our room at Canyon Village in the park, we got off the beaten path and had a great day of fishing on a small stream.

You, too, can enjoy the satisfaction fly-fishing brings on small streams. While the hordes of anglers flock to the more famous streams and rivers, you can fish some of the smaller, less-known streams and enjoy success.

It happened to Mike Manfredo and me as far away as the South Island of New Zealand. Mike and I flew to Christchurch on the South Island of New Zealand to experience a full month of some of the world's greatest fly-fishing. We fly-fished on some of the more famous streams and rivers for almost a week and were ready to quit and come home early. We experienced severe frustration, catching only two trout over twenty inches long—in the heart of some of the greatest fishing in the world. Then we decided to stay and fish the remaining three weeks, changing our strategy. From here on in, we'd fish some of the less-known trout waters on the island, many of them less than twenty feet wide.

Almost immediately Mike and I began to experience success. We fly-fished on small streams like Mistake Creek and a number of others that yielded trout up to twenty-five inches long. We hiked, boated, and flew to waters that were off the beaten track. Many of these small waters in New Zealand had even been avoided by the locals. On not one of these small streams did we ever encounter another angler. And yet we saw and caught huge trout.

Many of the most productive small streams I have fly-fished are those that have to be reached by hiking. I am certain there's a high correlation between the distance you have to walk to reach a stream and the productivity of that stream. Fish a high-quality stream next to a well-traveled road, and you'll probably have a less-than-average day. Go off the beaten path and hike a few miles to a stream, and you'll likely have a good day.

How do you get off the beaten path? Make an effort to search for those off-the-road small streams that most other anglers avoid. Look for those small streams that don't necessarily follow a road. Hunt those streams that you have to hike into. When you do, you'll experience the success of searching for productive waters and the great fishing that follows.

3.
Fishing Tackle and Gear for Small Streams

SEVERAL SMALL-STREAM enthusiasts, like Joe Dougherty and Greg Hoover, kept telling me about their exploits on these trout waters. After a year of listening to their success stories, I decided to become reacquainted with small-stream fly-fishing. I did almost everything wrong that first time out. I took my nine-foot Orvis Spring Creek graphite fly rod with me on an extended hike to a small stream. I hiked up over a mountain, down a steep cliff on the other side, and finally made it to the small stream. I hadn't seen this productive brook trout stream for more than twenty years.

No sooner did I start to fish than I gave up in utter frustration. I quit early that day and swore I'd never do that kind of fishing again. Why? That nine-foot rod hung my fly up one every branch and tree near the stream. I quickly realized that a six- or seven-foot rod would have worked much more effectively. If only I had properly prepared myself. If only I had known beforehand what constituted the right equipment to take on that small stream.

The twelve-foot leader I took with me also proved ineffective on that futile attempt. Miles from my other fishing gear, I learned that the leader I had brought was too long to cast with any accuracy on this small stream. What I would have given to have had a five- or six-foot leader with me! On this tiny stream casting clearance was at a premium. Every tree, bush, and patch of brush along the bank and

Tom Walsh fly-fishes small streams frequently. He prefers using a bamboo rod like the small Orvis bamboo show here.

overhead seemed eager to catch my fly. There's no way you can control and accurately cast a leader twelve feet long under most small-stream situations. In total frustration, I finally cut off about three feet of the leader tippet.

Small streams really do require different fly rods, leaders, and other equipment. You'll make your trip much more pleasant if you're adequately prepared—and if you're not properly indoctrinated, you might make your first trip to that small stream your last.

But the correct rod and leader are just starting points. You'll need to take topographic maps with you, insect repellent, and a dozen other items that can make your stay more enjoyable. We'll examine some of the items you'll need to consider.

Fly Rods

When I first started fishing on small streams more than forty years ago, I had no problem selecting a fishing rod. I owned only one—a steel rod that telescoped from three to seven feet long. When I fished a small stream, I pulled the tip section out so the rod would extend to six or seven feet—just about perfect for many of these smaller waters. This was my live-bait rod. I didn't start fly-fishing for another ten years.

Thankfully, those days of telescoping rods and live-bait fishing have vanished from my trout repertoire forever. For two decades after that episode I enjoyed using a Fenwick Fiberglass and several responsive bamboo rods. More than ten years ago I abandoned those for the new graphite. Graphite rods have gone through a series of radical improvements since first introduced. The new generation of graphite fly rods makes casting so much easier that I've discontinued using bamboo rods completely. Graphite rods make small-stream fly-fishing much more practicable. Small fiberglass rods also work effectively on those trips to small streams. Fenwick makes some great glass rods that are reasonably priced and work well in closed-in places.

Manufacturers produce graphite rods in so many sizes and actions that it's difficult to decide which are best for small-stream fly-fishing. How can you determine which is best for you? First, use one that feels comfortable to you. But further, select a rod that works well in the extremely tight situations you'll find on small streams. Test the rod for its roll-casting ability. God knows, you'll do more roll casts in a couple of small-stream trips than you've ever done before. The right small-stream fly rod will feel like a normal extension of your arm. Test

A typical Orvis graphite rod and reel designed for small streams.

the rod from a kneeling position and a prone position. I hate to be the first to tell you, but you'll be using these positions a lot on small streams.

What fly rod do I prefer using on small streams? Since that initial bout with an oversized rod and leader, I've relied on graphite rods from six to eight feet long with good stiff actions and designed for a 4-, 5- or 6-weight line. On occasion I'll get my 7½-foot Fenwick Fiberglass out and use it on some of the more enclosed small streams. A stiff-action rod helps when you have to resort to roll casting on these smaller streams.

I don't like the "midge" rods that were so fashionable a decade or two ago although I have several of these made of bamboo in rod lengths from 4½ to 5 feet long.

On rare occasions you'll meet an old-time fly-fisherman who uses a 10- to 12-foot dapping rod. Anglers crawl next to the bank, lift these long rods out over the stream, and follow their fly on a short line. This method works, but the rod is cumbersome.

Following are some examples of acceptable small-stream fly rods you might consider. Always stay with a brand name and a maker that stands behind its products.

Table 2: Small-Stream Graphite Fly Rods

Company	Model	Length	Line Weight	Rod Weight (ounces)
Orvis	8-Foot Western Midge	8'	#4	2.88
Orvis	Brook Trout	7' 6"	#4	2.50
Orvis	Small Stream Special	7'	#5	2.50
Sage	LL SERIES-GFL 473 LL	7' 3"	#4	2.13
Sage	LL SERIES-GFL 576 RPL	7' 6"	#5	2.63
Loomis	FR 783 IM6	6' 6"	#3	1.38
Loomis	FR 904 IM6	7' 6"	#4	1.50
Loomis	PMR 904F	7' 6"	#4	3.19
Cortland	395	7' 6"	#5-6	2.50
Cortland	476	7' 6"	#4-5	2.50
Cortland	693	7' 6"	#4-5	3.00
Winston	Trout Rod	7' 6"	#5	2.38
Winston	IM6 Trout Rod	7' 6"	#5	2.50
Powell	DF70-1	7'	#4-5	2.63
Powell	DF76-2	7' 6"	#5-6	2.63
Powell	Cedar Creek	7' 3"	#3-4	2.63
L.L. Bean	Double L	7' 6"	#4	2.25
Fenwick	Brushy Creek Rod	6'	#5	2.63

Orvis makes an ideal rod they call the Small Stream Special (Table 2). Orvis designed this 7-foot, 2½-ounce rod for a 5-weight line. It throws an extremely tight loop, and the action helps you get under low-lying logs and brush. Doug Truax, of the Orvis staff, also suggests the 4-weight 8-foot Western Midge and the Brook Trout (7½ feet for a 4-weight line). Tom Ackerman, of the L.L. Bean staff, recommends the Double L Dry Fly rod for those fly-fishing small streams.

R. L. Winston makes several rods that serve as ideal small-stream rods. The two I prefer are the IM6, 7½ feet for a 5-weight line, and a 7½-foot for a 5-weight Trout Rod.

Powell Rods makes two graphite fly rods that perform well on small

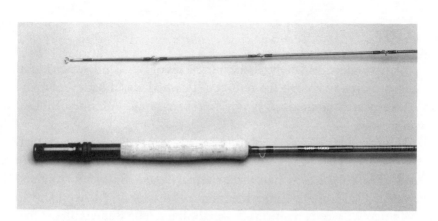

A Cortland rod designed to help you fly-fish on small streams.

streams. The Light Action comes in a 7-foot length for a 4–5 weight line. If you prefer a heavier action, you might choose the Medium Action Graphite in a 7½ foot length, designed for a 5–6 weight line.

Cortland also produces a small-stream rod you might consider. The company makes a 7½-foot GRF-1000 rod designed for a 5–6 weight fly line.

Sage has two rods which are ideal for small streams. The GFL 473 is a 7-foot, 3-inch rod designed for a 4-weight line, and the GFL 576 RPL is a 7½-foot rod for a 5-weight line.

Last, but certainly not least, G. Loomis has several small fly rods which will serve you well on small streams. Their FR 904 IM6 is a 7½-foot rod designed for a 4-weight line, and the FR 783 IM6 is a 6½-foot graphite rod designed for a 3-weight line.

To review, the type of fly rod many fishermen prefer for small-stream fly-fishing is a 6- to 8-foot graphite with a fairly stiff action and designed for a 5-weight line. Some small-stream afficionados use some of the newer fly rods with lines as light as a 2-weight. I prefer a heavier line. All the rods we discussed above perform well on small streams for some fly-fishermen. They cost from $90 for the Cortland 476 to over $300 for many of the others listed. You must make the final decision. Test several before you decide. Make certain you feel comfortable with your final selection on small streams. Remember, you'll use the roll cast many times on those small streams so use a rod that'll perform this cast properly.

Reels

I often wonder how I endured the intricacies of fly-fishing when I first began. Forty years ago the only reel I owned was a heavy, clumsy Shakespeare automatic. Try any finesse casting with one of those some time.

Now anyone can own a good single-action reel. Orvis suggests that you balance your Small Stream Special fly rod with a Battenkill 5/6 reel (Table 3). I also like the extremely quiet Scientific Anglers System Two-L reels. Either the model 45-LC or 56-LC works well with many fly rods requiring 5-weight lines. The Battenkill and the two Scientific Angler reels weigh between 4.1 and 4.8 ounces.

A lightweight gem for small mountain streams is the Hardy Featherweight. This small mountain special weighs in at only 3.5 ounces.

Don't overlook the new Martin LM 45. As fly reels go, it's relatively inexpensive, but it does a good job.

Loomis has an excellent reel that can be successfully used on small streams: the Model 345 (so named because it's designed for 3-, 4-, or 5-weight lines).

Most good single-action reels are expensive. The Battenkill runs

A good example of a small-stream reel.

around $75; Martin's LM 45, around $90. The Loomis 345, the Ross G1, and the Cortland 2100 cost about $150; and the System Two-L, Sage 504, and Hardy Featherweight, about $175. All, if treated properly, will last a lifetime.

Whatever reel you decide on, make certain it balances well with the rod you've selected. If you're a neophyte at small-stream fly-fishing, you would probably be wise to select a balanced rod-and-reel outfit. Go into any of your better specialty fly-fishing shops and have one of their reps help you select the proper gear.

One thing consistently irritates me about some fly reels. They don't always hold the fly line satisfactorily. The spools fill up, and the last few feet of fly line and leader are difficult to reel in. Make certain the reel you select adequately handles the backing, fly line, and leader.

Table 3: Some Reels for Small Streams

Company	Model	Diameter (inches)	Capacity	Reccommended Backing (20lb.)	Weight (ounces)	Line Weight #
Hardy	Flyweight	2 ½	DT4F	None	2.63	3 or 4
Hardy	Featherweight	2 ⅞	DT5F	None	3.50	4 or 5
Orvis	CFO III	3	WF5F	75 yards	3.25	3 or 4
Orvis	Battenkill 5/6	3 ⅛	WF5F	100 yards	4.13	5 or 6
Cortland	CRI Fly Reel	2 ½	WF4F	20 yards	2.70	4
G. Loomis	345	2 ⅞	DT4F	65 yards	2.85	3, 4, or 5
Martin	LM 45	3 ⅛	DT5F	25 yards	3.10	3, 4, or 5
Scientific Anglers	45-LC	2 ⅞	DT5F	30 yards	4.29	4 or 5
Scientific Anglers	56-LC	3 ⅛	DT5F	90 yards	4.46	5 or 6
L.L. Bean	Double L-#4	³⁄₁₆	WF5F	100 yards	3.25	4, 5, or 6
Marryat	MR-7	2 ¹¹⁄₁₆	WF5F	45 yards	3.50	5
Sage	504 L	2 ⁹⁄₁₆	WF4F	100 yards	3.38	3, 4, or 5
Ross	R1	2 ¹³⁄₁₆	DT4F	30 yards	3.14	3, 4, or 5
Ross	G1	3	DT5F	25 yards	3.60	4, 5, or 6

Leaders and Lines

That twelve-foot leader I referred to earlier would have worked great on a larger river. On smaller streams, however, use a leader from five to seven feet long. A leader this long will handle most of the dry flies, wet flies, and nymphs in sizes 12 to 18 and the streamers you use on a small stream. I have never had to resort to a longer leader. On occasion you will use a longer tippet up to eighteen to twenty inches. Here are several formulas I've tested for short dry-fly leaders:

Table 4: Short Dry-Fly Leaders

Diameter (inches)	Leader #1	Leader #2	Leader #3	Leader #4	Leader #5
.015	26.5"	18"	22.5"	12"	12"
.013	13.5"	12"	19.5"	12"	12"
.012		8"			12"
.011	14"		9"	12"	
.010		6"			6"
.009*	9"		5.5"	9"	
.008*	4"	4"	3"	9"	6"
.007*	21"	22"	16"	12"	12"
Total length	7' 4"	6' 10"	6' 3 ½"	5' 6"	5'

* Sections using the new super-strong leaders

Table 5: Tests with Various Length Leaders on Small Streams

Leader #	Short Casts			Long Casts (over 30')			Drag	Total
	Overhand	Sidearm	Roll	Overhand	Sidearm	Roll		
1	7	8	6	8	8	6	6	49
2	7	8	8	8	8	7	5	51
3	8	6	6	8	6	6	6	46
4	8	7	7	7	7	7	5	48
5	8	8	7	7	7	7	4	48

Comments

Last year I conducted experiments with five short leaders on small streams. I tested all of them on a small stream and rated them for their roll-casting and general casting ability. I used the same size-12 dry fly and fly rod with each and cast in the same pool. You'll see the results in Table 5. The higher the number in the chart, the better the leader performed.

I purposely constructed Leader Number 3 (Table 4) to be unlike any of the others. It didn't turn over as well as the others. Notice this leader contained a long butt section and a short tippet section. In this experiment with five dry-fly leaders numbers 2, 4, and 5 have the best ratings for the size-14 dry fly I used.

Try your own tests. Tie up a few of your favorite leaders and test them on a small stream. Make certain you vary the tippet diameter according to the size fly you plan to use. I usually use a .007-inch tippet for size-12, -14, and -16 dry flies. If you plan to use smaller flies, you may want to tie on a #006 or .005 tippet. If you plan to use a larger fly, your tippet might be .008 or .009. The ideal leader is a delicate balance between rod, line, and fly. When the tippet doesn't collapse but drops your pattern quietly on the surface with plenty of S-curves, you have the proper leader (see Chapter 4 for a more detailed explanation).

I prefer to use a stiff leader material like Mason or Maxima for the butt section and one of the super leaders like Dai-Riki, Umpqua, or Orvis for the tippet section. George Harvey, in *Techniques of Trout Fishing and Fly Tying* (Lyons and Burford, New York, 1990), agrees. He ties a stiff leader for the butt (.015 to .011), then a softer leader for the tippet (.009 to .007) section. On most occasions a .007 tippet will suffice. Leaders number 4 and 5 in Table 5 are a variation on his formula.

George Harvey has developed many leader formulas. His short dry fly leader might look like the following:

.017 - 5 inches ⎤
.015 - 12 inches ⎟
.013 - 10 inches ⎬ hard nylon   .008 - 6 inches ⎤
.011 - 10 inches ⎟   .007 - 9 inches ⎬ soft nylon
.009 - 6 inches ⎦   .006 - 16 inches⎦

This 6-foot leader, depending on the size and resistance of the fly, is an excellent one for small streams. George uses Climax for his butt section (hard nylon) and Umpqua or Cortland for the tippet (soft nylon).

On normal leaders on big water I like to use a tippet about two feet long, even longer, sometimes, when I want a lot of S-curves in the float. You can't afford that luxury on leaders for small streams. You'll note in some of the leaders above that the tippet is shortened to one foot. On some leaders I go up to eighteen inches with the tippet section. If you're matching a Trico hatch with a size-24 dry fly and you prefer a finer tippet, you can add a section of .006. If you do, cut back on the size of the .007 six inches. Try this tippet on a small stream. Note how it roll casts readily. You'll probably use the roll cast most often on small-stream fly-fishing so you need a short, responsive leader.

Even a 6-foot leader is too long on some smaller streams. Tie a shorter leader on one of your reels. Try the five-foot leader (Leader Number 5) I suggest above. Experiment until you feel comfortable with it. I use Maxima for the butt section of the 5-foot dry-fly leader and Dai-Riki for the .008 and .007. I said before that the tippet is quite short on this leader. To obtain a better drag-free float, you might prefer lengthening the tippet a couple of more inches. In more closed-in places you might go with the foot-long tippet.

If you prefer to use a nymph, wet fly, or streamer, you might want to go to a fairly short leader. Leader numbers 4 and 5 should make a good leader for most wet flies and nymphs. Orvis makes a good six-foot wet-fly leader called a Special Tapered Leader for Sinking and Sink Tip Fly Lines. This works exceptionally well in those small-stream situations. I've never seen a good ready-made six- or seven-foot dry-fly leader. If you like these short leaders, you'll have to tie your own.

If you're using a Woolly Bugger or streamer, cut back on the tippet length. Note that both leader formulas drop by .002-inch with each addition. Don't ever drop by more than that figure. If you do, you'll find that the tippet section often gets tangled around the butt section. Although I prefer using Maxima for the butt section, I run into a problem. I have difficulty finding diameters that only drop by .002-inch.

Joe Dougherty and Greg Hoover both fly-fish small streams extensively. Both have developed excellent small-stream leaders. Joe uses George Harvey's formula for a $10\frac{1}{2}$-foot leader (from his book, *Techniques of Trout Fishing and Fly Tying*), cuts it exactly in half, and has a completely satisfactory leader, perfect on small streams.

Experiment until you feel comfortable with the leader you've tied for small-stream fly-fishing. Remember to keep the leader short, and don't be satisfied with the leader you're using until you feel it works perfectly for you.

Make your butt section six inches longer than the formula calls for it to be. When you tie the butt section onto the fly line using a nail knot, you'll lose a lot of the heavier end.

Dropper

A dropper, which allows you to use two or more patterns at one time, is simply an extension of one of the leaders. If you're using a wet fly, you might want to add a dropper fly. When tying the knot between your last two leader sections, let the second leader (the thicker one) extend out about six inches. In other words, don't cut the second leader to the knot, but let it extend. In the example of leader material above, you'd tie on a foot-long piece of .009-inch stock, extending half of that beyond the knot. This half then becomes the dropper. Tie a fly on this dropper and one on your tippet.

Even if you don't plan to use a dropper fly, leave a couple of inches of this second leader extending. Tie a knot at the end of the extension and add the necessary lead shot to keep the wet fly, nymph, or streamer on the bottom. If you add lead shot to the dropper, and you get hung up on the bottom, you'll often lose the dropper and save the fly.

Leaders and drag

George Harvey has preached for years about the virtues of a perfect leader with a fairly long tippet to provide plenty of S-curves when the fly lands on the water. These S-curves help the fly float drag-free for a longer distance. George always said that if a fly-fisherman can create these curves in his line when he casts, he'll improve his chances of success by as much as 90 percent.

Even on small streams these S-curves help. On the final cast with the dry fly, stop the line short, bring the fly rod down with the casting arm, and hold the rod parallel to the water. Try this technique that George has spent a lifetime teaching. It will improve your chances of success instantly.

Fly lines

Fly-fishermen have a wide selection of fly lines available to them. Weight-forward, level, double-taper, sinking, and other lines produce a wide array of results. On few occasions will you require a sinking line on small streams. One or two split shot attached twelve to fifteen inches above the fly should reach the bottom with most nymphs, streamers, and wet flies on most occasions. A plain old double-taper floating line will most often suffice for most of the flies used. Most of my small-stream fly rods call for a number-5 line. I have a bias against fly rods that take lighter lines (numbers 3 or 4). These lighter lines don't roll cast as well on small streams.

Always buy a well-known fly-line brand. I've been burned many times thinking I saved money by buying an unknown brand of fly line, only to toss it away after trying it one time. Stick with names like Cortland, Orvis, or 3M, and you know you're buying quality. I use these three brands exclusively and don't even bother trying others.

To review, select a seven-foot fly rod with a good stiff action and one of the better single-action reels that balances well a 5-weight double-tapered line with a five- to seven-foot leader attached. Most of the time you can begin your leader with a piece of .015-inch stock for the butt and taper it down to .007. Use stiff leader material for the butt section and a more supple leader for the tippet. This outfit should satisfy most of your small-stream fly-fishing demands. But having the proper fly rod, reel, leader, and fly line are just the beginning—you'll need other gear for small-stream fly-fishing.

Other Gear You'll Need

Dry fly spray and line dressing

Dress your line thoroughly before you begin fly-fishing on a small stream. It's essential that you keep the line floating high on these waters. It's especially important if you plan to do a lot of roll casting. Carry spray or dressing for your dry flies since false casting is at a premium.

I usually use a hair dressing called Albolene. This makes fantastic fly dressing. A jar that costs about $6 lasts for five to ten years.

The better the tip of your fly line floats, the easier it is to roll cast. Umpqua makes a line dressing that lasts for an entire day of fishing.

Hip boots

I have a pair of felt-bottomed Ranger boots that have defied destruction. These ten-year-old boots have hiked to hundreds of small streams, almost stepped on several rattlesnakes, and have saved me from falling many times. I visit no small stream without them. Always take a pair of hip boots with you. If you plan to hike into a small stream, you might want to consider a pair of stocking-foot hip boots. If you plan to hike more than just a couple of miles, carry your boots in your backpack and put them on once you reach the stream.

Camouflage clothing

I once took a friend along with me to a small stream near my home. He wore a bright red sweater on that cool spring day. I recommended he shed that for a dark brown one I had. Do as much as possible to hide yourself from your wary prey. Use drab colors so you tend to blend in with the background. You'll need every advantage you can muster to catch streambred and native trout.

Polaroids

George Harvey called me upstream. He had spotted a heavy trout just out from a rock on the far side. He pointed it out to me, but I couldn't pick it out in the heavy shade. He gave me his clip-on Polaroids, and I immediately saw the fish. I now never travel to a small stream without my clip-ons. Make certain you take Polaroids with you when fishing small streams. You, too, will be able to see many more trout from a greater distance, and often you'll be better able to get into position to cast to those you see.

Insect spray

On one occasion I had to leave a small stream because I forgot my insect repellent. Carry a good quantity with you. It seems insects bite more readily on these small isolated streams with a heavy canopy. Before you ever begin to fly-fish, apply a generous amount. Try to have someone else apply the insect repellent, and try not to get any repellent on the patterns you plan to use. I'm convinced that if any gets on the pattern, it will lessen your chances of catching trout.

Compass

You'll probably wander off onto unfamiliar roads. A compass can help you maintain your sense of direction while in the car and while hiking to and from the stream. But just having a compass isn't enough. Learn how to use it!

Topographic maps

George Harvey always takes plenty of topographic and forestry maps with him when he plans to fish small streams. These maps show all state forestry land and are provided by the Pennsylvania Bureau of Forestry. These maps take on special importance when you wander onto dirt roads. Topographic maps help you locate branches or tributaries and new waters to fish. Don't ever try to find new streams without a good inventory of maps. In fact, topographic maps show which streams are intermittent during the summer and which probably flow all year long. Usually as I drive, George searches his maps for nearby streams we can fly-fish. Maps can help you determine how large a stream is and how fast it flows without your even seeing the water. (See also in Chapter 2, Locating Small Streams.)

You can purchase topographic maps from many sporting-goods stores, your county extension service office, or from the U.S. Geological Survey (USGS) Map Sales, Denver Federal Center, Box 25286, Denver, Colorado 80225 (tel. 303/236-7477). Also check with your state forestry department or the local office of the U.S. Forest Service (USFS). The USFS publishes topographic maps of national forests, and many state forestry departments also publish excellent detailed maps.

pH-tester

A pH-tester is not a necessity, but it can be extremely helpful. If you plan to fly-fish new water or trout streams in other states, a device that

Tom Walsh uses a pocket-type pH tester to check the acidity on a small stream. By using this device you can find tributaries or branches that pour mine acid or acid rain into the main stem.

tests the pH of the water can mean the difference between a good and a poor day of fishing. The pH-tester checks the acidity or alkalinity of a stream. Streams registering below pH 7.0 are normally considered acidic; the lower the number, the more acid the water contains. Streams registering above 7.0 are considered alkaline; the higher the number, the more alkaline. Limestone streams normally register between 7.5 and 9.0. By carrying a pH-tester with you, you'll see firsthand the ravages of acid rain and the effects it can have on the environment.

Most highly productive small streams will register a pH between 6.0 and 8.0. Streams with a pH lower than 6.0 appear to hold fewer aquatic insects. Scientists have found that the number and diversity of insects decreases rapidly as the pH drops below 6.0.

We all complain that streams don't hold the number of trout they once did. Further, many of us, including me, blame part of the demise of trout populations in small streams on acid rains. In an earlier chapter I suggested that you consistently record the pH of all the small streams you frequent so you have an idea how well these streams are holding up to acid rain.

Using a pH-meter or tester can also help you locate those small streams which contains some buffer. Some branches or tributaries hold a pH above 7 while the main stem struggles to register a 6. Look for these branches, and fish just below them.

Until a few years ago if you planned to test the pH of a stream, you had to take a lot of gear with you. You used either a heavy meter or litmus paper. You couldn't take the meter very far, and the paper gave inexact readings. Just recently digital pH-testers have arrived on the market. They're not much larger than a small flashlight and usually give readings with an accuracy of plus or minus 0.2 unit. You check the accuracy of these devices with a buffering solution. Some of your better fly-fishing stores now stock these digital pH-testers. They range in price form $25 to $50.

Thermometer

Many years ago I fly-fished a small tributary of Mehoopany creek in northeastern Pennsylvania. The main stem produced plenty of beautiful brook trout. One day I decided to hike up a productive-looking branch. I felt certain no one had been on this tributary this year. I hiked upstream a half mile to a fish a pool formed from a ten-foot high waterfall. What a spectacular scene! The water seemed to have a tannic-brown color to it so I checked the temperature. It felt warm to the touch. In the midmorning sun the thermometer produced a 69-degree reading. I didn't fish but hiked up the branch for a good mile before I saw an opening in the woods. Here was a five-acre beaver pond on the branch. I scanned the water and saw chain pickerel and

Terry Malloy carries a backpack or day pack with him on his hikes into remote small streams to fly-fish.

sunfish swimming near the breast of the dam. The dam had been in place for years.

Always carry a thermometer with you on your trips to locate new small streams. Check the water temperature on these streams before you fish them. By checking the temperature and the pH, you can get a good idea how healthy the stream is. It might save you from a frustrating experience.

Hemostat

Native trout often take artificials viciously. It's important to use barbless hooks and a hemostat to extricate hooks that have been taken deeply.

Day pack

George Harvey and John Randolph carry small packs sometimes called "day packs" with them when they hike to small streams. In the bag they place items like flies, lunch, maps, compass, and a thermos. You can add things like a first-aid kit, survival kit, stocking-foot hip boots, a pH tester, and other items.

When fly-fishing many of the small streams of the West like northeastern Nevada's Cave and Duck creeks, always carry water with you. Much of the water in northern Nevada emanates from small, cool, pure springs that you can drink from directly—but if you're not certain of the quality and purity of the water, always carry some with you. After a day of fly-fishing some of these small alder-lined streams, you'll crave water. Often you fish in an environment with a humidity less than 10 percent.

First-aid kit

Ten years ago Rick Wolfe and I fly-fished a small stream in northern Pennsylvania. This was Rick's first time fly-fishing, and I wanted to show him a good time. We descended a steep bank to approach the small stream we had selected. On the rocky decline Rick fell headfirst into the stream. His hand hit against a large boulder and began to bleed profusely. Although the wound didn't look deep, we headed back for the car and to the emergency room of a local hospital. The three-mile hike back to the car and the twenty-mile drive to the hospital took us almost two hours. Since that time I carry a first-aid kit with me on all those long hikes to small streams.

Many of the small streams you'll fish will also be miles from any medical facility. Be prepared for minor emergencies. You might also want to take a snake-bite kit with you. The survival kit I recommend below contains many of the supplies you'll need for an emergency.

Survival kit

My son, Bryan, and I had hunted grouse for the past three hours near Sixmile Run on the Allegheny Plateau in central Pennsylvania. Now we headed back to the car. We hiked for a half-hour and saw nothing familiar. Darkness set in. We were hopelessly lost. Where was the

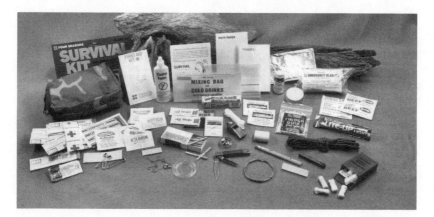

Try to carry a survival kit with you on long hikes into inaccessible, remote small streams. The kit should include first-aid and other items necessary to survive if you get lost or injured.

car? Where was the stream where our car was parked? I told Bryan we'd walk for another fifteen minutes and if we saw nothing recognizable, we'd make camp for the night. No use thrashing through the woods in the dark. What would we do? How could we build a fire without matches? Just as we were ready to stop for the night, we came upon a dirt road which finally led us to our car.

Since that incident I have always carried a survival kit with me on long hunting trips and on hikes to fish small streams. Oak Norton of the Four Seasons Company, at 1857 Park Forest Avenue, State College, Pennsylvania 16903, makes one of the best kits I've ever seen. It contains everything you'll need when you're fly-fishing small streams. The survival kit includes bandages, pins, razor blades, antiseptic pad, nylon blanket, compass, knife, water tablets, and much more. The kit even includes fishing hooks. Place the kit on your belt or in your day bag, and make certain you carry it with you.

Walking or wading staff or stick

I like to carry a walking stick or staff with me on small streams. Purchase one that folds so it isn't bulky. Sometimes you'll encounter rocky streams. I always carry the stick or staff also to ward off any snakes I see along the stream.

Four-wheel-drive car

Both George Harvey and I drive four-wheel-drive cars. On many of your trips off the beaten track, you'll find yourself on unimproved dirt roads. A four-wheel-drive car helps. Make certain it has a high enough clearance. You'll travel many rock- and boulder-strewn dirt roads.

Last, but not least, let people know where you're fishing. When you plan to hike into small streams or take roads into unknown areas, make certain someone knows where you're going. It's not common, but I've been known to get lost for a couple of hours.

4.
Tactics and Techniques
for Fly-Fishing
Small Streams

AH, WHAT A beautiful small stream! In front of me four native trout rose in a small boulder-strewn pool. A thick cluster of alders lined the far bank. A heavy hemlock grew next to the stream on the right side. I stepped behind the evergreen tree to hide from the trout and began casting to the closest rising fish. I made two or three false casts before I attempted to place the fly just upstream from the feeding fish. Before the fly landed on the surface, it tangled in a hemlock branch just upstream from me. I quickly freed the fly from the tree. All four trout still rose. I hadn't scared them with my mediocre casting technique. I began casting to the same trout—this time an overhanging alder on the left bank seemed to reach out and take my fly.

What a frustrating day! With almost each cast the fly landed in a tree or in brush near the stream. I hadn't prepared for casting in such close quarters.

Once you become adept at fly-fishing small waters, you'll automatically survey a stretch of water before you approach it and begin planning your strategy. You'll look to both sides, in front of you and behind, to see what, if any, clearance you have. You'll start thinking which cast will work on this section as you arrive. You'll decide where to stand, creep, or crawl so you can best reach the pool or riffle.

Look around before you decide what type of cast you'll use. Remember that on many small streams you'll encounter debris, trees, bushes, and brush throughout.

When I became reacquainted with small-stream fishing, I had to change many of my ways of thinking. On medium-to-large streams and rivers I paid little attention to my approach to the stream. On Henry's Fork in Idaho, the McKenzie in Oregon, even the Beaverkill in New York, I didn't keep a low profile but waded below rising trout and cast upstream to them. I didn't look to the left or to the right for obstructions—there were none. But tactics and techniques change drastically when fly-fishing small streams.

George Harvey cautioned me on my first several approaches. Initially I casually walked to the stream and attempted to cast into an area not bigger than a bathtub. Almost immediately I spotted trout darting upstream, downstream, under banks, but always away from my fly.

After correcting my early mistakes, I approached small streams cautiously, almost always from a crouching position. One of the first decisions you have to make as you approach a section to fish concerns the best position on the bank or in the stream to cast from. George watched the first few times and also encouraged me to stay a good distance from the stream and to remain concealed. Often I'd cast as far as thirty to forty feet away from the stream to prevent scaring the native trout. Part of my fly line lay on the stream bank. Almost immediately I began to catch more of these wily trout. The approach to the stream and the ability to keep a low profile determine who will and who will not consistently catch native trout. Crawl, creep, or slither to your casting position near the stream. Stay prone if you think any further movement will scare the trout. Always scan the area to determine from what location you will best be able to reach the trout in the section of stream you're fishing.

Before you attempt too many of the tactics and techniques that I suggest, you might want to try some of them on your lawn at home. Move up and down the lawn prepared to cast from a squatting position. Practice this position because it'll be one of your favorite stances on most small streams. Practice all the casts I suggest later in this chapter. You'll use a lot of unusual ones.

Finally, set up targets on the lawn and cast to them. Accurate casting is extremely important on small streams. You might get one chance with one cast before you scare all the trout in a pool. Pretend that first cast in the pool will be your only cast.

If you have brush and trees handy, practice by placing them around the area to which you plan to cast. Try to cast over, around, and under the brush you have in place. Spend plenty of time trying to cast around these obstacles. God knows you'll be confronted with many when you actually fly-fish on small streams. The sooner you get acclimated to this type of environment, the better off you'll be.

The Approach to the Stream

As you approach a section of water you plan to fly-fish, look around and keep asking yourself some questions. Where are the trees and bushes? Are they overhead, just above the stream? Is there an opening near your casting position? Is there an obstruction in back of you? What type of cast will you make? A roll cast? A sidearm cast? Or, maybe there's enough clearance overhead and behind that you can cast overhand. If you decide on a roll cast, what type do you use? Study each pool and riffle before you begin casting and decide which casting technique is best for that section and where to cast from. Look along the banks. Is there any brush in the water? Are there any rocks or boulders in the pool? Where will the trout most likely lie? Can you best fish the water from above, the left side, the right side, or from the bottom of the area? What type of cast will cover the water adequately? Are there bushes on both sides and right up to the stream? Where will the trout lie in the pool: at the riffle at the head of the pool, at the tail of the pool, or in the pool next to a rock?

As part of the approach, you've got to decide how you're going to keep hidden from the trout. Can you hide behind a rock, bush, tree, or other object while casting? Does the layout of the section you're fishing require that you actually crawl up to the stream?

Another extremely important aspect of the approach is your movement toward the streams. Vibrations from your motion alert native fish quickly. Trout not only see you but also feel your movement.

I stated before that on many occasions I've had to crawl on New Zealand streams for thirty to a hundred feet to approach the stream without spooking the trout. In fact, anyone who wants to fly-fish small streams in the United States should try fly-fishing large streams and rivers in New Zealand before he starts here. It was on the upper end of the Waikaia, on the South Island of New Zealand, that Mike Manfredo and I had the terrible first week mentioned earlier. In the entire week we caught maybe a half-dozen trout over a foot long. What happened? Where were all the lunkers everybody talked about? They were there, but we had to change our tactics.

Mike and I decided to fish these crystal-clear New Zealand streams and rivers as you'd fish many small streams found in the United States—from a prone position. We both noticed that when a hatch appeared, the trout fed freely. However, when we approached the water, the feeding frenzy ended quickly. Even when we crawled and crept to the water, the trout were very suspicious. We finally decided to employ tactics used in army basic training when you have to crawl under barbed wire while machine guns fire live ammunition above you. From an almost motionless prone position, Mike and I cast our flies over a rising trout. Then and only then could we consistently take New Zealand trout. The pristine waters in that country are so clear that trout notice any movement.

Remember, your approach to trout on small streams is critical. Use any type of obstruction nearby to block your approach from the trout. If nothing's nearby, then crawl on all fours to a casting position. Once near the stream and ready to cast, you must decide whether you will cast from a prone position.

As you move into an area, you've also got to think of the type of cast you want to make. If there are obstacles behind and overhead, a roll cast might be the best type. If there's clearance overhead and then behind, a regular overhead cast might be best. Maybe the stretch you're planning to fish has no clearance overhead, and none behind you, and just a foot or two above the surface. Then try a sidearm cast just above the water. Maybe the only way you can get the fly to the surface of the pool you want to fly-fish is with a bow-and-arrow cast. After several days of fly-fishing on small streams, you'll begin developing a plan and asking yourself some of the questions I suggested.

As you move upstream, study each pool and pocket to get into the best casting position. If you prefer using a wet fly, streamer, or nymph, you'll probably move downstream searching for the best angle from which to cast. Occasionally you'll have to approach a pool from the upstream side even with a dry fly.

When you finally get into position for the initial cast into a promising section, try to make your first cast as accurate as possible. Often on the first cast to a productive-looking pool I've hooked a bush on the far side and frightened away any trout in the area.

Don't make many casts into an area. Trout in small streams will move an inordinate distance to take an artificial. George Harvey always says that three or four casts in an average pool of a small stream are plenty.

We said earlier that you'll make some of your casts from a crouching or prone position. Often you'll creep fifty feet or more to get to a good casting area. You'll often remain in this crouched position until you leave that section. You'll make many of your roll casts, sidearm casts, even your straight overhead casts from a bent position.

Several years ago I fly-fished a small stream with another fisherman, John Gordon. John and I leapfrogged upstream alternating fishing and watching. John consistently does well using spinners on small streams. One day several years ago he caught more than a hundred trout on one stream in an afternoon of fishing. The day the two of us fished, I used an ant. In some pools I picked up two and three trout on flies. Usually after John caught one fish, no more struck his spinner. It appears fly-fishermen have at least one advantage over spinner and bait fishermen in late summer.

Remember, if you catch a trout on the first cast in a section, cast several more times into the same area. On many occasions I've caught two and three trout from the same general section of a pool or pocket. If you're careful, you can, too.

Casting from a Distance

I just related what happened on a large pool. I stopped short of the bank and began casting. On many other occasions you'll find yourself thirty to forty feet away from the stream attempting to cast to a diminutive pool that's out of your view. I remember George Harvey coaching me one day on casting over grass to a pool thirty feet away. Most of the fly line lay on the grass, and only three or four feet of the leader tippet made it all the way to the pool. I couldn't see the fly but heard a violent splash, set the hook, and moved toward the stream bank to release a ten-inch brookie.

Again, it takes practice to accomplish this type of cast. It's an unusual feeling when at first you see all your fly line lying out of the water.

Preventing Drag

On many occasions you'll see trout swirl, strike short, or just plain miss your artificial. Often they do that because drag has set in on the fly—in other words, the fly is drifting slower or faster than the water in which it is floating. "What?" you say. "It's difficult enough to get the fly into a good area without getting hung up in a bush." With exceptionally short five- or six-foot leaders, you'll get more drag than with those nine- to twelve-foot leaders you normally use. With larger leaders you can afford to construct a tippet that's two feet or more long. On small-stream leaders, you have to sacrifice tippet length. If drag continues to be a problem on small streams, add a longer piece of tippet material. In some of the leaders we listed in Chapter 3, you might want to lengthen the tippet to eighteen to twenty inches.

George Harvey taught me a handy way of preventing drag. If your fly is floating in slow water, then make certain your butt section is also floating in that same slow water. Mend your line by lifting the butt to the left or right so it floats in water moving at the same velocity as the water that floats the tippet. Conversely, if your fly is floating in fast water, then make certain your leader butt and fly line float in that same fast water.

Don't forget the S-curves when casting. The more S-curves you create when your tippet lands on the surface, the longer the float, drag-free, your pattern gets.

Setting the Hook and Landing the Trout

Once you've tricked a trout into taking a fly, you might have difficulty setting the hook. Don't forget, you're fishing in sort of a tunnel, and on many sections of small streams you'll scarcely have room to lift the rod tip to set the hook. That's why it's so important to continuously maintain a tight line, almost at the expense of drag. Remember at all times that the area where you can lift up on the rod is extremely limited. I don't care to remember the number of times I lifted the rod to set the hook and hit the limb of a tree.

But the battle has just begun. If the trout is any size, it has a distinct advantage over you—it knows the stream well—much better than you do. The quarry knows all the logs, bushes, undercut banks, trees, and boulders. George Harvey recently hooked a heavy fifteen-inch brown trout on one of our favorite small streams. The two-pound brown headed directly toward the far bank and a network of roots undercutting the shoreline. George realized where the trout was heading and gave a gentle but firm nudge on the line to head the fish downstream away from the entanglement. The trout responded to George's firm hand. Always survey banks and other obstacles where hooked trout will run. Figure out beforehand what strategy you'll use to keep them away.

Types of Casts

Often after I fly-fish small streams for a good number of days consecutively, I long for those large, wide-open streams and rivers. I've fly-fished the Beaverkill in New York's Catskills for more than twenty years. Very seldom have I had to resort to the unusual casts required on small streams. Very seldom have I had to rely on a roll cast or a cross-body cast. Never on larger streams like the Madison in Yellowstone Park have I had to depend on the bow-and-arrow cast or the change-of-direction cast. But if you fish long enough on small streams, you will use all of these casts and many you invent yourself. You'll never realize from how many angles you can roll cast until you get on challenging sections of small streams. Let's look at some of the types of casts you'll use.

Bow-and-arrow cast

Many times on small streams you'll encounter areas with little or no room to cast: no room behind you, no room overhead, no room to the right or left to make a cast to a productive section of water. Maybe, just maybe, however, you have a narrow opening extending from you to the part of the stream you want to reach. Perhaps this is where you can try the bow-and-arrow cast—through that narrow imaginary tunnel.

The bow-and-arrow cast is simple. Fold the leader up to the fly line.

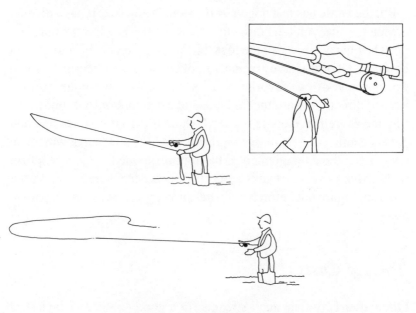

Figure 4.1 Bow and Arrow Cast
1. Grab the fly and line in your left hand (if you're right-handed).
Insert: point the barb of the hook away from you.
3. Bend the rod by pulling back on the fly and line and let the fly go
toward your target.

Grab the fly, leader, and fly line between your thumb and forefinger. With the same hand, bend the rod back toward you. Aim the bow (rod) toward the spot where you want the fly to land. When you let go of the fly, it should alight on the surface near where you wanted to fish.

Practice the bow-and-arrow cast before you attempt it on the stream. After a few futile attempts, you'll wonder how you fly-fished on small streams without using this technique. Keep your other hand out of the way, and watch how you hold the fly so the hook doesn't get caught in your hand when you let go of it.

Before you test this type of cast on a stream, try it in your backyard. Experiment with a fly that doesn't have a point and practice with it until you feel confident on the stream. Try this cast for a whole morning on your next trip. It's unbelievable how accurately you can place a fly on a small, tightly enclosed stream using the bow-and-arrow cast, and in time you'll be able to do so with a finesse that will scare few native trout.

Don't expect the bow-and-arrow cast to carry the fly more than ten or twenty feet. Use the cast when you have no room above or to the sides to move the fly rod.

Roll cast

The West Branch of the Clarion River in northern Pennsylvania holds a good number of trout throughout the season. It contains a productive two-mile stretch of catch-and-release water. The landowner in this stretch of the stream will not allow any wading or fishing from the west side. Any fly-fisherman is seriously limited in his options on this small river. In most cases his only option other than the normal overhand cast is a roll cast.

Consider what happened recently to me on a nearby small stream. George Harvey dropped me off and told me to work my way upstream a half-mile to the car. It was the first time I had fly-fished this small stream. The water presented a problem that I hadn't encountered previously. Directly behind the stream on both sides ran a ten-foot-high bank. I attempted to backcast several times but each time got caught in brush on the high bank. I began lifting the line back toward me on my right-hand side, then rolling it back upstream along the surface—roll casting. It worked well—I didn't get caught on the backcast. On occasion, where there was some clearance to my back,

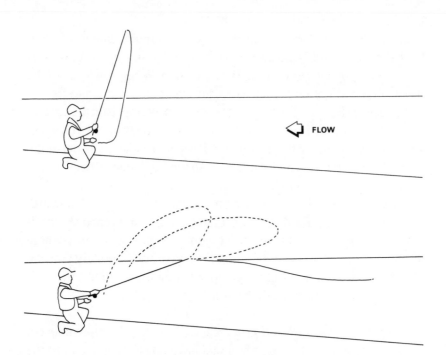

Figure 4.2 Roll Cast
1. Bring the fly line toward you.
2. With a strong forward motion lay the line toward your target.

I'd false cast once or twice to dry the fly between roll casts.

I used the roll cast almost exclusively upstream for a half-mile. I noticed that when I used this method of casting, I could get the dry fly under upstream brush and bushes much more easily than I could with an overhand cast. You can manipulate the roll cast well on these small streams, especially if you're using a five- to six-foot leader.

The roll cast is one of the easiest casts to learn and one of the most practical for closed-in small streams that you'll ever use. Study the diagrams and practice it repeatedly until you've mastered it. For a more effective roll cast, make certain that you've dressed your line so it floats. When the fly line sinks, it is much more difficult to roll cast.

If you're right-handed and find that you don't have room to roll cast on your right side, you can backhand roll cast from your left side. Try it several times and see how easy it is to do. Bring the line up to you on your left side and roll the line upstream with the rod.

Side roll cast

We just explained the roll cast under ideal conditions usually found on larger streams and rivers. On many smaller streams, you won't have the luxury of bringing the rod completely upright for the roll cast. More often than not you'll find yourself stooping or crouching when you're roll casting. Seldom do you have the luxury of standing erect and roll casting. On many of these creeks you won't have anywhere near the room you require to perform an orthodox roll cast.

What do you do? Hold the rod to the right or left just above the water if you have some clearance there. Roll the line with the rod upstream from the position just above the surface. Work with this type of roll cast—you'll be amazed how well it works on those enclosed streams. The line stays near the water and enables you to place the fly under tight places. You might have to shorten the tippet to get the roll cast under some of those obstructions.

Experiment with underhand roll casts, sidearm roll casts, backhand roll casts, and every other type of roll cast from almost any angle to supplement your arsenal of tactics and techniques for small-stream fly-fishing. If you're right-handed, practice making roll casts with your left hand.

Flipping

Often when you're fly-fishing on small streams, you'll have no other way of casting than holding the fly in the left hand (if you're right-handed) and flipping the fly upstream to a predetermined spot. Bass-fishermen have used this tactic for years and call it "flippin'." They use a long rod and a short cast. It works for trout-fishermen on small streams, also. There's no rolling the line on the water—no false casting above you—just a simple cast holding the fly in your left hand. This cast often works when there's no overhead space and no room to roll cast. It is so simple that it is often forgotten by many anglers as a last resort for covering a pool or pocket on a small stream.

Sidearm casting

How many times when you're fly-fishing small streams will you encounter productive water with no room overhead to cast? How

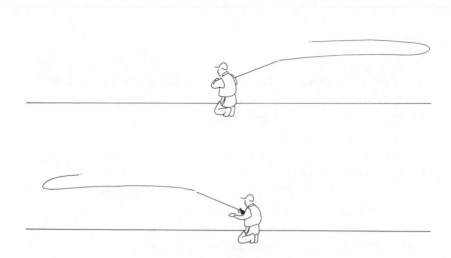

Figure 4.3 Sidearm Cast
1. False cast the line downstream parallel to, and a few feet above, the surface. If the stream is to your right and you're casting upstream, you can often use the sidearm cast. If the stream is to your left and you're casting upstream, you can often use a cross-body or backhand cast. With the latter, you false cast the line with the right hand parallel to, and a few feet above, the surface, but on the left side of the body. If you're left-handed, you would use the cross-body cast when downstream is to your right and you're fishing upstream. 2. Set the fly down with a slack-leader cast (to provide S-curves) by stopping the rod short.

many times will you see a foot or two of clearance just above the water's surface? What type of cast is best under these conditions? Maybe a sidearm cast. Think of casting like pitching in baseball. From time to time you'll find a need, especially on small streams, for a cast that's lower than an overhand cast. Sometimes you'll use a three-quarter cast; other times, a sidearm; and other times, almost an underhand cast. All can be useful when you encounter brush, bushes, and trees.

Examine the accompanying diagrams. Deciding when to use a sidearm is all part of the total decision-making process as you first inspect a section of water.

Backhand or cross-body casting

As I waded upstream on the right side of the stream, I spotted a productive-looking pocket and undercut bank on the far right. Heavy brush prevented me from casting by conventional right-handed methods directly behind me, but there was plenty of room to my left. What could I do? Use the cross-body cast.

On many occasions in dense cover you'll be unable to cast overhand, sidearm, or underhand. On those occasions you might try a backhand or cross-body cast. If you're a right-handed caster, cross-body casting means casting with your right hand from the left side of your body. The cast might be overhand, sidearm, or underhand, but backhand casting often works when other types of casting fail. The cross-body cast seems foreign to you until you've done it a few times. Then it becomes another weapon in your arsenal.

Change-of-direction cast

I arrived at a highly productive pool. Two hefty brook trout rose at the upper end to a sparse but lingering hatch of Blue Quills. Blue Quills had appeared on the water that mid-April day shortly after noon and continued to appear for more than four hours. I tied on a size-18 dry fly to match the hatch. How was I going to cast the fly and get it up to the trout? There was no room overhead to cast. Only a narrow opening

Figure 4.4 Change of Direction Cast
1. False cast in the direction of the opening (perpendicular to the stream).
2. On the last cast, aim the line upstream to its final destination.

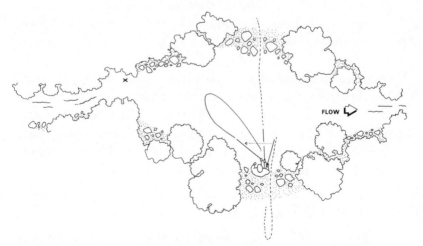

went from left to right across the stream, a ninety-degree angle from where the trout rose.

This called for a change-of-direction cast. I cast the fly from the right to the left in the narrow opening above the pool, then made a forceful move with my hand to position the fly at the head of the pool. It worked: the fly landed just a foot above the lower-rising trout! The change-of-direction cast in that pool helped me catch two trout that would have been impossible to catch without it.

Practice with this cast several times. False cast the line in one direction; then when you're ready to deliver the fly to an area, change directions with the final cast. You'll be surprised how easy it is to utilize this type of cast and how many times you can use it, especially on small, enclosed streams.

Dapping

Fishermen, especially those who have fished for a number of years, often use a method of fishing in which they touch the surface of a stream with a live insect. They call that "dapping." Fly-fishermen on small streams sometimes resort to dapping when every other kind of cast fails. On some sections of some small streams, if every other type of cast ends up in a bush or tree, try dapping. Strip out two to three feet of line and lift the fly to the spot you want to fish. Drop the fly on the spot and follow it downstream with the tip of the rod. Pick up the fly and place it on another section of water and follow it downstream as far as it floats drag-free. Although dapping works well in extremely tight places, the motion of the rod may often frighten wary trout. A short four- to five-foot leader seems to work best when you're dapping.

Myron Culbertson, of Mill Creek, Pennsylvania, has a great rod-building reputation. On occasion he makes beautiful ten- to thirteen-foot fly rods for small-stream fly-fishermen. These accomplished anglers use his long rods to dap on small streams. They use no fly line, only monofilament on the reel. They move from pool to pool, extend the elongated rod over the pool, and wait for a strike.

Casting with your other hand

I cast right-handed. Several years ago I broke my right wrist in a softball game. The break happened in early June, and I had a cast on the arm for six weeks. How was I to fly-fish? I began casting with my left hand. It took a while, but after several days it felt comfortable. For the remainder of the fishing season that year, I used my left hand for casting. You'll discover on small streams that sometimes it is more convenient to place the rod in the left hand and cast. Try casting with your other hand. Practice doing it on larger water. Cast with a short line and see how quickly you adapt. Being ambidextrous can help under heavy brush conditions, especially where you don't want to or can't cross the stream.

False casting

The practice of casting several times before placing the fly on the water's surface—or "false casting"—becomes a luxury one can ill afford on many small streams. Too many fly-fishermen spend too much time false casting and too little time with their pattern on the water. I've often watched fishermen false cast five or ten times when two or three would do. Remember, the longer that fly floats on the surface, the better your chances of catching trout.

On occasion you'll encounter times when a weak, false cast is all you can achieve. Try more, and you'll invariably get hung up in the brush, bushes, or trees. Grease up the dry fly adequately, make the one weak false cast, and place the dry fly on the surface. Later you'll see some patterns that I recommend to help you keep false casting to a minimum. But sometimes you have to dry off the fly, and there's no room at the stream to do it. Look around you. Is there an opening nearby where you can go to false cast several times? Is there a trail, path, or road near the stream? Move to that opening, make a few false casts to dry the fly, and return to the stream to cast.

Varying your Tactics with High or Low Water

Last year Bill O'Connor, a member of a private fishing club, invited me to fly-fish on his club's waters in early May. The visit that early-May Saturday had been preceded by a week of heavy rain. Even the small mountain stream flowing past the camp ran several feet above normal. Bill suggested I head up one of the small tributaries on the club's private grounds. Even this branch ran a foot or two above normal.

As I arrived at the first pool upstream, I wondered what pattern would be appropriate. No dry fly would work on these swirling torrents. I decided to go with a large black Woolly Bugger tied on a size-10 hook. I replaced the leader on my reel with a 5½-foot one with a .007 tippet. I attempted to cast the wet fly, but decided to place two heavy lead shot a foot above the pattern. Now, would the heavy wet fly sink? No strikes in the first pool.

I headed upstream and started dapping, or lifting the weighted-fly up and down, in the slow backwater of a gurgling pool. Within seconds a heavy native brook trout took the Woolly Bugger. I lifted the trout up over the high bank and began dapping again in the same eddy. A second trout hit the pattern.

I worked my way upstream a mile before I heard the dinner bell beckoning me back to camp for lunch. In that stretch of heavy water, I caught a dozen trout. Had I not added weight to the Woolly Bugger adequately and gotten it down to the bottom, I'm certain the morning would have ended in failure.

I had an opportunity to return to the stream in late August of the same year. No rain had fallen on the watershed for almost five weeks. When I arrived at the pools, I was amazed at the low water level a few dry months had produced. Pools three feet deep in May now barely had six inches of water in them at their deepest point. As I approached the first pool, two trout scurried under a rock. I couldn't get within thirty feet of the water without scaring the fish. What to do now?

I immediately changed the leader by adding a longer, finer tippet. Still the trout darted ahead of me in every pool. What pattern should I use under these low-water conditions? I tied on one of George Harvey's Deer-Hair Ants with a piece of pink fluorescent material to make it more noticeable under the heavy summer canopy.

Upstream a half-mile, where the raging torrents of a few months ago were replaced with low, clear water, I literally crawled up to the next pool. This same high, rock-ledged pool yielded two heavy brook trout in early May. I dapped the ant just over the ledge while I kept out of sight. I couldn't see the pattern on the water, but I did see a ring on the surface and set the hook. I lifted a seven-inch brookie up over the four-foot ledge, then on to the next pool where the same method brought a trout about the same size.

Why is all of this important? Small streams change drastically from early spring until late summer. Western small streams also vary. Visit some of the small streams flowing from the Kootenai Mountains in western Montana in June, and you'll see these flowing well above normal. Fly-fish these same streams in early September, and you will see unbelievably low, clear creeks. Fish them properly either time of the year, and you'll catch plenty of native cutthroats.

Let's look at the preparation for both high and low water on small trout streams.

George Harvey, Ben Williams, and I fly-fished a small, productive tributary to Young Woman's Creek recently in mid-June. Rainfall in the watershed totaled almost ten inches for the month of June. Young Woman's Creek spilled over its banks that day. Fly-fishing was out of the question with the high water. All three of us tried to decide what we should do.

"Let's try a small tributary," George said, "it always runs off quicker."

We headed downstream to the branch and headed up this tributary three or four miles. "We can use dry flies on this," George said, and the three of us headed in different directions on the branch. Remember, small streams clear up faster and provide good fly-fishing quicker after a rain.

George proceeded to present a "fishing clinic" on this small branch. In almost every pool and pocket he picked up one or two brown or brook trout. Most of the trout ranged from ten to twelve inches long. Ben and I stood back and watched George in amazement as he caught trout after trout on a dry fly in the high runoff.

A month later George and I headed back to the same branch, but this time there was one big difference: the water level had lowered by a foot or more. Low slow rapids replaced the high rushing rapids of June. Trout in the slower pools reacted much more quickly to any angler movement. In a section where George had caught a dozen trout just a month before, he now caught one. Was it the lower water? I think it was.

Late one September George Harvey and I traveled to the Kettle Creek watershed to fly-fish some streams George hadn't fished for many years.

We stopped in Cross Creek, and George reminisced with Charlie Cross, a lifelong resident of the Kettle Creek valley. George worked with Charlie back in 1937, 1938, and 1939, when George had obtained a grant to study native trout in the small mountain streams of north-central Pennsylvania. Out of those three summers of fishing came some excellent studies on trout in the watershed.

After reminiscing for an hour or so with Charlie Cross, George and I headed for one of his favorite haunts and one of the areas he used back in the late '30s, Trout Run. We drove upstream three or four miles until we hit one of George's favorite tributaries, Green Branch. When we crossed the bridge where the branch enters Trout Run, George commented that he had never seen the stream that low. Each pool we approached contained a half-dozen trout that darted from one end to another as we came close. A half-mile upstream the stream went underground. Above that only a dry streambed represented what was once a productive small native trout stream.

These low-water conditions provide an excellent time to check your favorite small streams—when stream flow is at its worst. For the next few years that section of Green Branch that went underground would have few trout in it. Yes, some would move upstream or downstream in the spring runoff, but it might be better to avoid this area and fish upstream where the water reappeared.

Many limestone streams go underground part of the summer. I can think of a dozen streams that flow beneath the streambed in August and September. I've checked the insect life on these sections in April and May and found very few aquatic insects in them. It also should follow that few trout will be found there even when water flows above ground.

High-Water Preparation

Patterns

Carry patterns like the Woolly Bugger, Green Weenie, or Green Worm, and streamers like the Lady Ghost on those early-season trips and whenever you encounter high water. You'll probably need some weight to keep even sizable patterns deep. I prefer to add weight to the body of the fly when I'm tying it. If you don't have that opportunity, add several shot to the leader to keep the pattern near the bottom on those high-water trips. Start with one or two shot and add more if the pattern doesn't reach the bottom. There's nothing more frustrating than a day on a raging small stream without any success because you're not getting the fly deep enough for trout.

If you prefer to remain with dry-fly patterns, make them fairly big sizes on those high-water occasions. Carry Coachmans in 12s and 14s. If you tie your own patterns, tie in two high-quality hackle to make the pattern more buoyant.

Complement your high-water selection with some large stonefly nymphs that copy the common *Pteronarcys*. This genus contains species that inhabit small streams in all parts of the United States.

We indicated earlier that many small western streams flow high through spring and early summer. Add to this that many of them enjoy a temperature of 40 to 55 degrees during that time, so large weighted flies are extremely important.

When Mike Manfredo and I fly-fished a small stream called Mistake Creek on New Zealand's South Island recently, we fished for two days without any success. What made us keep coming back? On each of those hikes up the canyon leading to the the upper end of the stream, we spotted several rainbows over twenty-five inches long. Mike had tried for them the past two days without success. He now came back with a weighted Woolly Bugger. He caught a twenty-six-inch rainbow with that weighted pattern on his first attempt the third day. Mike had added plenty of weight, and the lunker took the Woolly Bugger on the bottom of the five-foot-deep pool.

Leaders

On those days with high water, don't worry about the size of the tippet—a .007 is plenty small enough. Often I use a leader no longer than five feet in high-water conditions.

Tactics

No need to creep or crawl to pursue your prey under high-water conditions. Often you can fly-fish next to the stream without frightening the trout. Don't overlook the slower backwater or eddies. In high-water conditions trout often lie in this slower water.

In high-water settings, you'll find yourself fly-fishing from the top of the pool with a large wet fly, twitching the pattern upstream. Place the fly in the fast water at the head of the pool, and feed line out so the pattern drifts downstream.

You'll also dap a large streamer or dry fly when waters run high on small streams. Drop the streamer and let it sink to the bottom. Gently lift the pattern up and down. Try it in one area a couple of times, then move onto another section of the slow water. Trout, especially brook trout, often hit a large wet fly presented this way.

Types of streams to fish

During one entire summer, every time George Harvey and I planned to fly-fish Young Woman's Creek, we found it in flood stage. On several occasions we attempted to fish it but soon left, tired of fighting the high water. Each time, we ended up on a smaller branch or tributary of Young Woman's where the water, although high, was fishable; and, each time, we experienced success on these smaller branches. Don't give up if the small stream you plan to fly-fish is too high. Look around for smaller branches and tributaries.

Low-Water Preparation

Patterns

Late-summer, low-water fly-fishing calls for an abrupt change in patterns on small streams. Small ants and beetles replace large clumsy patterns like the Woolly Bugger and Lady Ghost. Anglers use smaller patterns (sizes 14 to 20). Larger sizes in low water often put trout down. Don't forget to try attractor patterns like the Patriot and the Wulff Royal Coachman. Tie some of these attractor patterns on size-16 to -20 hooks.

Tactics

What a tremendous change in tactics the small-stream angler devises when the stream lowers and the pools become clear! Trout that earlier allowed you to walk within a few feet now scurry for cover in late summer under low-water conditions. Now crawling, creeping, and even lying prone on the ground are in order. Even the movement of the fly rod scares these native fish. Often it's best to exclude these streams from your plans in late summer until after a heavy rainfall occurs.

You'll have to depend on many of the casts we talked about earlier under low-water conditions. The bow-and-arrow cast, roll cast, side-arm cast—you'll resort to these and others to catch trout. And many of them will have to be performed from a half-prone or prone position.

Don't forget those small tributaries to larger, more marginal streams and rivers. When these larger waters warm up in the summer, concentrate on small, cooler branches for some excellent late-season fly-fishing. Many of the trout you catch near the mouths of these larger streams in the East will be planted fish that have survived most of the fishing season.

Leaders

The leaders we suggested you use earlier might not be long enough for low-water conditions. If you don't have any success with those listed, add another twelve to eighteen inches of tippet material. If all else fails—you know the stream contains a good supply of native trout, and you feel you've stayed appropriately far enough away from the stream, and you still can't catch trout—lengthen the leader to 7½ feet and change the tippet to one with a diameter of .006 inch.

Types of streams to fish

Remember those small tributaries and branches we discussed earlier under high-water conditions? Forget them when late summer appears. Many of them barely run with a trickle, and those trout still in those branches live under trees, banks, and rocks.

Concentrate on some of the small streams with plenty of water and a sufficient number of hiding places to hold a reasonable trout population. Predation from birds and mammals is at its peak in the summer, so make certain the stream you fish has undercut banks and obstacles to hide the native trout.

We've discussed a lot of tactics and techniques that you should find useful on small streams. Now get out on your favorite small stream and practice.

5.
Hatches on Small Streams

HUGE MAYFLIES EMERGED upstream and downstream. These greenish-winged insects struggled desperately, trying to become airborne before a nearby trout snatched them. A pool upstream that had seemed void of trout just a few minutes earlier came alive with brown and brook trout crazily chasing sluggish duns. The trout seemed to lose their timidity. I could wade much closer to rising trout than under no-hatch conditions on this stream. Even a poor cast brought results on this small, productive stream during this heavy hatch of Green Drakes.

The sporadic hatch began shortly after noon the last week in May and lasted for more than four hours, with duns appearing and trout rising all afternoon long. I lost count of the number of trout that took my three mangled imitations of the drake. What a day to be on a small stream! A great hatch with many rising trout, many of them stream-bred! And not one other angler within sight! What else could a fly-fisherman ask for?

Fish this same Green Drake hatch on a larger stream like Penns Creek, and you might come away totally frustrated. I can't remember the number of times I fished this hatch on a large stream and quit in despair while thousands of duns and spinners still floated on the surface. Some trout seemed to ignore the dun and spinner and feed on the emerger; others fed on another insect and totally ignored the Green Drake. Try this same hatch on small streams, and see what happens.

Not too long ago George Harvey and I fly-fished another small mountain freestone, this time in late April. The high, cold, spring water seemed to hold few trout. George and I picked up an occasional trout prospecting, but neither of us saw any trout rise. Only one thing kept us on the water well past noon. This small stream as well as many others throughout the country holds an exceptional early-season Blue Quill hatch. This *Paraleptophlebia* species, *P. adoptiva,* usually appears in late April near 1:00 PM. These mayflies can stand quite a bit of fast water, so you'll likely encounter this hatch on many of your favorite fertile small streams.

George and I drove to a pool that we thought held plenty of trout and waited for the hatch to appear. Soon a few, then hundreds, of size-18 Blue Quill duns struggled on the surface. At least a dozen trout rose in front of George in a twenty-foot-long pool. George quickly picked up ten trout and yelled for me to come upstream to sample the same success he had. Soon I caught another five trout out of the same pool. Trout still rose to Blue Quills at 3:00 PM. George and I finally sat back on the bank and reflected on our fine day on this small stream. What a day! What a hatch!

Another small stream nearby holds a tremendous Sulphur or Pale Evening Dun hatch. The hatch appears nightly for five to six weeks every year. These mayfly spinners fall just at dusk, and trout feed voraciously on the spent-wings. The fall is so dependable that I take lots of fishing friends to this small stream to enjoy this very predictable hatch. Through every night in June and early July, you can expect to fish over trout rising to a spinner fall.

Do some of your favorite small streams contain some decent hatches? Examine the nymphs in the stream. Do you see a lot of the same type? Do you see some nymphal shucks (the outer skin the nymph sheds when it appears as an adult) on rocks or in the water? Look at some spider webs near the stream. Do they contain a good number of adult aquatic insects? Check also any puddles near the creek. Are there any dead mayfly spinners in these pools? By looking all around you near the stream, you'll deduce effectively the kind and quantity of recent hatches on the water.

A hatch of mayflies, stoneflies, or caddis flies on a small stream activates trout to surface-feed. Where there was no previous activity, now there is plenty. As you fly-fish more regularly, you'll see that certain insects are found more often on small streams than are others. We'll examine some of the more common insects in their order of appearance from February to October. (Table 6 lists insects found on small streams in chronological order.)

Common Small-Stream Insects

Western March Brown

Mike Manfredo, Ken Helfrich, and I had just finished fly-fishing on the McKenzie River near Eugene, Oregon. We'd experienced a fantastic hatch from 2:00 to 4:00 PM; the three of us caught more than fifty trout. This Western March Brown appears daily for more than three months on the McKenzie.

The next afternoon I headed back to Portland to take a plane back East. I had several hours to kill so I stopped a few times at small streams. At one, not more than twenty feet wide, I saw the same great hatch, the Western March Brown, that I had witnessed the day before.

This mayfly inhabits many small coastal and near-coastal streams in Oregon and Washington. It is a very unusual mayfly. It often begins appearing as early as late February on east-central Oregon rivers and streams and continues to appear daily in midafternoon until late May. If you're fortunate enough to find this species on one of your favorite waters, you're in for some great fly-fishing.

What a pity Oregon's fishing season doesn't take advantage of this great hatch! The Oregon season usually starts around May 1—eight weeks after the hatch begins.

Little Blue-Winged Olive Dun

What a spectacular hatch I met on a small mountain stream! It appeared in mid-April, and duns of the species emerged for more than two hours that afternoon. The hatch was the very common Little Blue-Winged Olive Dun *(Baetis tricaudatus)*. This species is one of a handful that is found on many streams of the East, Midwest, and West.

But wait! The Little Blue-Winged Olive Dun has more than one brood per year. I later found out that the Little Blue-Winged Olive Dun copied by a size-20 imitation reappeared on the same small

The Little Blue-Winged Olive Dun appears several times a year on many small streams of the East, Midwest, and West.

stream in October. On both occasions when I matched the hatch, I caught trout on this small imitation. *Baetis* species inhabit both small and large streams. The same imitation that you use in the East can match the same hatch in the Midwest and West.

Sometimes the April hatch of this species appears a size larger than later hatches. Carry imitations in sizes 16 to 20 to effectively copy the Little Blue-Winged Olive Dun. Don't overlook the nymph of this species. A size-16 Hare's Ear fished in the riffles where these mayflies emerge can catch a lot of trout during a hatch. Fish the nymph a couple of inches under the surface.

We said the Little Blue-Winged Olive Dun has more than one brood per year, so you might see the hatch in March and April, again in July, and sometimes as late as September on into late October. The hatches in fall can produce a bonanza feeding frenzy—the last one of the year. Look for the Little Blue-Winged Olive Dun on many small streams during late-fall afternoons.

Blue Quill

Blue Quill imitations copy at least a half-dozen different mayfly species all in the genus *Paraleptophlebia*. These species first appear in the East and Midwest in late May and continue with different species appearing throughout the season. The insects appear in the

One of the first heavy hatches of the year on small streams in the East and Midwest is the Blue Quill.

morning or afternoon. On western rivers there are at least four prominent mayflies copied by the Blue Quill. Most of these species in the East, Midwest, and West frequent small streams. I talked earlier about the earliest hatch in the East and Midwest, *Paraleptophlebia*

A late season Western Blue Quill (Paraleptophlebia memorialis) *that appears on many small Western rivers and streams.*

adoptiva, and how it produces some heavy hatches even on small streams.

Take plenty of size-18 Blue Quills along with you on your trips to your favorite small streams.

Quill Gordon

The Quill Gordon is the first relatively large mayfly of the season in the East. A size-14 imitation appropriately copies the natural. The insect appears in mid-April on very pristine waters like those often found in the upper reaches of many of our larger streams. The hatch most often appears in the afternoon.

Hendrickson

The Hendrickson and Red Quill copy another early-season species which most often appears a couple of days later than the Quill Gordon. You'll find the Hendrickson on many of the smaller streams in the East and Midwest. A size-14 Red Quill copies the male, and the Hendrickson, the female. Hatches occur on small streams usually in midafternoon. Many of the small tributaries of the Au Sable in Michigan and the Brule contain the Hendrickson hatch.

You'll find the Hendrickson on many of the smaller streams in the East and Midwest.

Sulphur and Pale Evening Dun

I had a half-hour of light left. Earlier on this mid-June day I noted that several spider webs near the stream contained plenty of Pale Evening Duns *(Ephemerella dorothea)*. Some of these duns still struggled futilely to free themselves of the trap. I knew they had just emerged the night before. I waited at the bottom of a deep pool with a sizable run at its head because Pale Evening Duns often emerge in the rapids. Within minutes duns appeared at the head of the pool and where no trout had risen before, four now took up feeding positions. Three of those took my size-18 Pale Evening Dun before I left.

The Pale Evening Dun *(E. dorothea)* begins on eastern and midwestern streams in early June and continues to appear nightly into late July, inhabiting many small streams in heavy numbers. If you find a hatch with this species, you're in for some good fly-fishing in June.

Anglers often group several important mayflies in a loose group they call Sulphurs, Pale Evening Duns, and Pale Morning Duns. Sulphurs *(Ephemerella rotunda* and *Ephemerella invaria)* are usually copied with a size-16 pattern; the Pale Evening Dun *(Ephemerella dorothea)* with a size 18; and the Pale Morning Dun *(Ephemerella inermis* and *Ephemerella infrequens)* with a size-16 or -18 hook.

Always carry plenty of Sulphurs in sizes 16 and 18 when you fly-fish on small streams in the East and Midwest. The counterpart to this species is imitated by the Pale Morning Dun in the West in a size 16 and 18. Many of the spring creeks of the West hold heavy Pale Morning Dun hatches *(Ephemerella infrequens* and *E. inermis).* The limestone creeks of the East also harbor a good supply of Sulphurs *(Ephemerella rotunda* and *E. invaria).*

Sulphurs *(E. rotunda* and *E. invaria)* most often appear on eastern and midwestern waters evenings from mid-May to late June. Pale Morning Duns can be found on western waters in the morning and afternoon from the end of May into late July on some streams and rivers.

March Brown

Lift up the rocks in many of the small streams of the East and Midwest, and you'll find only one large dark brown nymph clinging to the rocks—the March Brown. The nymph and adult provide an important food source for trout on many smaller streams. Adults emerge sporadically from late morning through early evening. I've seen heavy March Brown hatches emerging in creeks no wider than ten feet. The natural is a sizable one imitated by a size-12 artificial.

Look for this important small-stream species from mid-May to mid-June throughout its range. Since the dun appears sporadically throughout the day, if you find a small stream with a good population, you can match the hatch for several hours over rising trout.

Green Drake

Dave Landis lived for several years near Helena, Montana. He fly-fished and guided on many of the streams and rivers in that area of the state, including many of the smaller waters. He recently relocated back to Pennsylvania. Two years ago Dave came upon a Green Drake hatch on a small stream called Dick's Run. "Imagine my surprise," Dave said. "In a stream barely two feet wide and a few inches deep there were dozens of Green Drakes hovering above the water. I would never have guessed that they inhabit such small water."

The Green Drake does inhabit many small streams. When you hit this hatch on a small stream, you can imagine what can happen. The

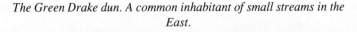

The Green Drake dun. A common inhabitant of small streams in the East.

Green Drake seems almost partial to many small eastern streams. Sure, it's found on Penns Creek in Pennsylvania, the Beaverkill in New York, and the Savage River in Maryland—but the same large mayfly also frequents many small waters throughout its twenty-state range. Often when you find this large (size 10 to 12) mayfly on small streams, it appears all day long. If you're fortunate enough to meet the hatch, you can often fly-fish to rising trout for hours on end. Look for large native trout to feed when this bonanza appears.

Look for the Green Drake in mid-May in the southern range; in late May in Pennsylvania and New York; and early June in New England. Normally on large streams and rivers the hatch appears near dusk. On small streams, however, the hatch can appear sporadically all afternoon and early evening. If you're fortunate enough to meet this hatch and have an appropriate imitation, you're in for some fast action.

Blue-Winged Olive Dun

The Blue-Winged Olive Dun pattern in sizes 14 to 18 copies several closely related species found throughout the United States. Hatches begin in late May in the East and Midwest with the appearance of *Drunella cornuta*. These mayflies usually appear from late morning through early afternoon. A western species *(Drunella flavilinea)* emerges in June and July.

Chocolate Dun

Few anglers have ever matched a hatch of Chocolate Duns. Yet, many small streams in the East and Midwest hold sporadic hatches of this mayfly. Look for the hatch in late May around noon. The spinner fall can be important to match in the evening.

Dark Green Drake

My son, Bryan, and I sat down by a small stream in central Pennsylvania. We took time out for lunch and sat by a 150-foot-long pool created by a family of beavers. Shortly after noon we noticed a few, then hundreds of large mayflies emerging in the deep slow pool. These mayflies, Dark Green Drakes, appeared a size or two larger than the massive Green Drake. Trout began to feed on this late-May emerger and continued to feed all afternoon.

The Chocolate Dun and Spinner (shown here) emerges sporadically throughout the day on small streams.

You'll find the Dark Green Drake on many small streams in the East and Midwest in late May and early June.

The Light Cahill appears sporadically in late May and early June on many small streams.

Recently I encountered another hatch of Dark Green Drakes on the last day of May. I saw hundreds of huge duns emerge from 1:00 to 3:00 PM on a small, isolated stream. I invited George Harvey and Greg Hoover to experience this hatch the next day on this fifteen-foot-wide creek. By 2:00 PM these size-8 adults appeared on every slow pool on the stream. I tied on a huge (size 10, Mustad 94831) copy of the natural with deer-hair wings and began casting. On the first cast a native brook trout barely six inches long hit the pattern. I caught a half-dozen trout on that massive imitation during the hatch.

The Dark Green Drake is one of the largest mayflies you'll encounter. You can tie the imitation on a size-8 long-shank hook, and the pattern won't be too large. These sizable mayflies normally emerge on cold mountain streams with some slow water. Hatches of this huge mayfly begin around the end of May. You can see this insect emerging from noon until evening.

Light Cahill

The name Light Cahill is given to several species found on small streams. Seldom have I seen a concentrated Light Cahill hatch. Rather, these mayflies appear sporadically in the afternoon and evening from late May through June.

On small Colorado and Montana streams and rivers, you'll see hatches copied by a Light Cahill in July and again in early September.

Red Quill

Members of the genus *Cinygmula* often frequent small cold streams of the West. One commonly called the Red Quill *(Cinygmula ramaleyi)* is found in midsummer on many small streams around noon. Many of the tributaries to Rock Creek, near Missoula, Montana, including Welcome, Alder, Wyman, and Grizzly creeks, hold good numbers of this species. In a sampling of species in the Rock Creek drainage, only four of fifteen sites did not hold the *Cinygmula* species.

Slate Drake

Look at exposed rocks on some of your favorite streams in midsummer. Do you see some dark nymphal shucks of large mayflies on them? If you do, then your small stream probably contains a decent hatch of Slate Drakes. There may be several species of the common genus *Isonychia* inhabiting the stream. These fairly large mayflies often appear nightly for weeks on end in the summer. If the small streams you frequent have hatches of this group of mayflies, a size-14 Slate Drake will be especially effective.

Trico

Mike Manfredo, Craig Shuman, and Don Rodriguez of Fort Collins accompanied me to the Phantom Canyon on the North Fork of the Cache la Poudre River in northern Colorado. Thanks to the Colorado Nature Conservancy this preserve is open, on a limited-reservation-only basis, to the public. We hiked down a canyon path for more than a half-hour before we reached the fertile river below. As we arrived at the open meadow, we were greeted with one of the heaviest Trico hatches I had ever witnessed.

Tricos appear on thousands of streams and rivers throughout the United States. They appear on rivers as large as the Missouri, McKenzie, and Madison in the West—and on streams not more than fifteen feet wide. Tricos can be found on some smaller limestone and freestone streams. The lack of a heavy canopy appears to be an important requisite for the hatch. Even small streams which contain fairly open areas can harbor this important mayfly species.

Most of these insects are copied with artificials in sizes 20 through 24. You'll need two patterns, since male and female spinners are dissimilar.

Tricos appear in the East, Midwest, and West from mid-July until the first heavy frost in September or October. Look on your favorite small streams from mid-July to late September for the Trico. If you fly-fish small limestone streams flowing through meadows or small mountain streams with interrupted canopies, you might find the hatch.

Western Green Drake

If you're fortunate enough to hit one of two species that make up the Western Green Drake, you're in for an eventful day of fly-fishing. Hatches appear sporadically on many of the small western streams just before noon and continue well into the afternoon. *Drunella (Ephemerella) grandis* with its three subspecies frequents many of the small streams of the West. The other common Green Drake, *Drunella doddsi,* can also be found in June, July, and August.

Little Blue-Winged Olive Dun
(Western species)

Baetis bicaudatus frequents many of the smaller streams of the West. One of the most common Little Blue-Winged Olive Duns, it is the same one found in good numbers on Henry's Fork. *Baetis bicaudatus* contains a body much more olive than its sister species, *B. tricaudatus.* If you plan to fish western small streams in July and August, carry some of these bright olive patterns tied on size-20 hooks with you.

Caddis flies

I had just flown a couple of thousand miles to fly-fish some of the great Montana rivers like the Yellowstone, Bitterroot, and Kootenai. I traveled up to the upper end of the Clark Fork near Anaconda in western Montana. The river here was no larger than many of the small streams in the East and Midwest. Not long after I started fishing, I witnessed one of the heaviest aquatic insect hatches I had ever seen. Thirty trout chased the food supply in front of me.

Guess what? A mayfly didn't cause this feeding furor. A size-16 Dark Brown Caddis was the culprit. I picked a copy from my fly box and proceeded to catch a couple of dozen brown trout that evening. Yes, even on small streams and rivers in the West, caddis flies can be important to imitate.

Lift up some rocks in your favorite small stream. Look for small slender tubes attached to these underwater stones. These tubes harbor larvae of caddis flies and are common on small trout streams in all parts of the country. Look at the backwaters and eddies on some of your favorite small streams. You'll probably see many caddis cases made up of several twigs glued together. Many of these *Brachycentrus* species frequent small streams. Take plenty of downwing caddis imitations in sizes 12 through 18 and with body colors of black, brown, green, tan, and gray with you.

Caddis flies make up an extremely important part of the food supply for trout. In a study of seven effluents in western Pennsylvania, Jan L. Sykora conducted a study for the U.S. Army Corps of Engineers, Pittsburgh District, entitled "Adult Aquatic Insects of Reservoir Outflows in the Upper Ohio River Drainage Basin," and found 111 different caddis species, many of these in heavy numbers. In *Trout Streams* Paul Needham reported that this aquatic order of insects makes up more than 43 percent of the aquatic foods taken by native brook trout. That number ranks extremely high. Caddis flies represented only 9.5 percent in brown trout and 18.7 percent in rainbow trout. You can see from these observations that native trout on small streams depend a great deal on the downwings, caddis flies. This seems to indicate that if you plan to fly-fish on small streams, especially for brook trout or rainbow, you should be prepared with a supply of caddis fly imitations.

Stoneflies

Stoneflies are exceedingly common and important as a source of food for trout on small streams. Some of the members of this order of insects can withstand more acid in streams than can other aquatic orders. Smays Run on the Allegheny Plateau flows no wider than five feet at its widest point. This small stream carries natural acid from peat bogs in the area. Yet this creek contains a fair population of the Giant Stonefly of the East, *Pteronarcys dorsata*. The thirty-millimeter-plus

Table 6: Small-Stream Emergence Chart

Imitation	Hatch It Copies	Dates	Time of Day	Size	East, West or Midwest
Western March Brown	*Rhithrogena morrisoni*	March to June	Afternoon	14	West
Little Black Stonefly	*Capnia vernalis*	March 1 to Apr. 30	Morning and afternoon	18	East, Midwest
Little Blue-Winged Olive Dun	*Baetis tricaudatus*	April 1 (2–3 broods a year) and September 15	Morning and afternoon	20	All
Blue Quill	*Paraleptophlebia adoptive*	April 12 to May 10	Afternoon	18	East, Midwest
Quill Gordon	*Epeorus pleuralis*	April 15 to May 10	Afternoon	14	East
Hendrickson	*Ephemerella subvaria*	April 20 to May 10	Afternoon	14	East, Midwest
Grannom	*Brachycentrus* species (Caddis fly)	April 20 to May 20	Afternoon	14 to16	East, Midwest
Sulphur Dun	*Ephemerella invaria and rotunda*	May 10 to June 30	Evening	16	East, Midwest
March Brown*	*Stenonema vicarium*	May 15 to June 10	Morning and afternoon	12	East, Midwest
Green Drake	*Ephemera guttulata*	May 18 to June 20	Evening (often in the afternoon on small streams)	10	East
Blue-Winged Olive Dun*	*Drunella cornuta*	May 20 to June 30	Sporadic, late morning	14	East
Dark Green Drake*	*Litobrancha recurvata*	May 20 to June 15	Afternoon and early evening	8	East, Midwest

* Spinners of these species appear on the water in the evening.

Imitation	Hatch It Copies	Dates	Time of Day	Size	East, West or Midwest
Chocolate Dun*	*Eurylophella bicolor*	May 25 to June 15	Late morning and afternoon	16	East, Midwest
Light Cahill*	*Stenacron interpunctatum canadense*	May 25 to June 30	Afternoon and evening	14	East, Midwest
Pale Evening Dun	*Ephemerella dorothea*	May 30 to July 15	Evening	18	East, Midwest
Little Green Stonefly	*Isoperla imbecilla*	June 1 to July 15	Day	16	East, Midwest
Giant Stonefly	*Pteronarcys dorsata*	June 1 to July 1	Evening	6	East, Midwest
Red Quill	*Cinygmula ramaleyi*	June 1 to July 30	Late Morning	16	West
Slate Drake	*Isonychia* species	June 1 to Oct. 31	Evening	12 or 14	East
Yellow Stonefly	*Isoperla bilineata*	June 1 to July 20	Day	14	East
Blue Quill	*Paraleptophlebia memorialis*	July 1 to Sept. 1	Morning	18	West
Trico	*Tricorythodes atratus, stygiatus,* and *minutus*	July 15 to Sept. 15	Morning	24	All
Blue Quill	*Paraleptophlebia guttata*	June 15 to Aug. 31	Morning	18	All

* Spinners of these species appear on the water in the evening.

adults of this species can be seen laying their eggs for the next generation in early June on Smays Run. Can you imagine what a feast just one of these adults or one nymph would give to the native brook trout population in the stream?

Stoneflies prefer very pure water like that found in many of these mountain streams. In June you'll also find the Little Yellow Stonefly and the Little Green Stonefly appearing throughout the day on many of these little streams. A size 16 copies the yellow insect, and a size 16 or 18 copies the green one. Don't fish those small streams in the East, Midwest, or West without plenty of stonefly imitations.

Don't overlook the stonefly nymph. If you check some of the rocks in your favorite small streams, you'll see some of these aquatic larvae. Tie up some of the more common forms for your area. Try fishing your favorite small stream sometime when a hatch appears. If you match the hatch, you're in for a memorable experience.

6.
Fly Selection for Small Streams

A BEAUTIFUL POOL lay in front of me. I had just hiked for an hour to a wild trout stream and eagerly assembled my gear. I sweated profusely from the 80-plus air temperature and the long hike. I scanned the surface to check for mayflies, stoneflies, caddis flies, or midges. I saw no insects on the water or in the air. No trout rose in the pristine, boulder-strewn pool. The area seemed void of trout. What pattern should I tie onto the tippet?

What pattern you finally decide to use depends on the water level, the time of year you're fishing, whether a hatch appears, and other factors. Of course, your preference comes into play. If you've had plenty of success with a particular pattern, why change? Although I have found that the majority of anglers who fly-fish small streams prefer dry flies, you might prefer to go underwater with your favorite pattern.

On that hot summer afternoon fishing trip, I selected a terrestrial as my first choice. I tied on a black Deer-Hair Ant and began casting. On the first cast the ant landed in a deep, fast riffle formed by a small tributary that entered the main stem a couple of feet above. I couldn't see the fly but almost immediately saw a heavy trout make a splash at my terrestrial. I set the hook too late. A few more casts in the same area and another miss. I had difficulty picking out the dark pattern in the heavy shade.

I hunted through my fly box for something brighter than the black ant. I selected another ant pattern that George Harvey had given me. This terrestrial looked like the one I had just cut off my tippet but with one major difference. George had tied a bright orange feather on the backside of this one. I thought I'd give it a try. At least it would be easier to see under these low-light conditions. I caught more than a dozen brown and brook trout using that terrestrial with the bright feather. More important, I missed only a couple. The bright fluorescent feather on top of the pattern improved my ability to follow the fly on the water and set the hook when fast strikes occurred.

I fly-fish heavily shaded small streams dozens of days throughout the season. One of my first considerations when I select a fly on these streams is how well I can detect that pattern on the surface.

What else should you consider in choosing a dry fly for small-stream fly-fishing? If you're dry-fly-fishing, select a pattern that floats easily with a minimum of false casts. False casting on a small stream is often a luxury that even experienced fly-fishermen can ill afford. Put Gerke's Gink or another floatant on the dry fly, make one or two false casts if you can, and start fishing. Many times you'll find that the only type of cast you'll be able to use with any effectiveness is a roll cast. Often I find myself walking away from the stream to a nearby opening, making a few false casts there, and returning to the stream.

You'll probably carry patterns other than terrestrials with you to your small-stream destination. You'll find that during June, July, and August attractor-type patterns work well. Under high-water and early-spring conditions, you'll possibly use streamers and nymphs. Woolly Buggers have saved the day for me on many occasions, even in midsummer. I've hit small streams after July thunderstorms and caught plenty of native trout on the Woolly Bugger. When the waters run deep, I often tie the Bugger on a short leader no more than five feet long. I lift the pattern into some of the eddies and dap it up and down in that slow water. Even though the water might be a foot or two high, you'll often do well with the Woolly Bugger and the dapping technique.

When you meet a hatch on one of these small, pristine streams, you don't want to be without a good pattern to match that hatch. Trout lose their timidity, and you'll see many of these natives chasing naturals.

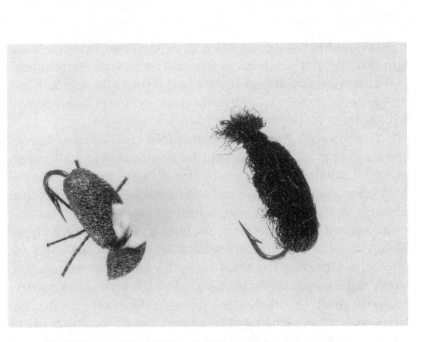

The beetle is an excellent choice on many small streams.

We'll look at some of these patterns like attractors, terrestrials, streamers, and patterns to meet the hatches.

Terrestrials

Before you fly-fish on that small stream, take some time out and observe the world around you. Look at that oak tree that recently fell across the stream. See those ants crawling on that fallen tree? If you look closely, you'll see dozens of black ants scurrying around near the stream. Toss one of these ants on the surface and see the water come alive. If you look long enough, you'll probably see some insects that strayed onto the water's surface.

Check the area a few feet away from the stream. You'll see beetles and crickets on the trees and bushes and under the rocks next to the water. Many of these land-borne insects accidentally get blown onto the surface of small streams. Trout feed on these and other terrestrials every day of the summer, especially when no aquatic insects of any kind appear on the water.

Beetles, ants, grasshoppers, crickets, cicadas, and caterpillars make up a majority of this windborne food that anglers call "terrestrials."

What terrestrials will work best for you? If you're fly-fishing in July or August and there's no hatch on the stream, you'll probably do well with an ant or beetle.

In *Trout Streams* Paul Needham lists food types taken by various species of trout. In his study he says that beetles made up 15.4 percent of land-inhabiting forms taken by native brook trout. Needham's book places paramount importance on terrestrials as a source of food for trout, especially trout in small, isolated streams.

Anglers still argue whether or not trout take copies of the Gypsy Moth caterpillar. George Harvey has used copies of this critter for more than a decade. The black caterpillar imitation, on occasion, works well, especially during May when the caterpillars are still relatively small. On other occasions, when the caterpillars become larger, trout won't even look at the pattern. Carry some copies of this species with you. You'll find George's tying description in the next chapter.

If you're fly-fishing a small limestone stream that meanders through a meadow, a grasshopper imitation might prove effective during the summer. I know the grasshopper pattern has saved the day for me on Colorado's Arkansas River and its tributaries. If you see the terrestrial on or near the stream, try an imitation of it.

The following are some productive terrestrials:
　Ant
　Beetle
　Cricket
　Grasshopper
　Caterpillar
　Cicada
　Bees and wasps
　Green inchworm

You will find the tying directions for many of the terrestrials in Chapter 7.

Attractors

Lloyd Williams, of Dallas, Pennsylvania, has fly-fished small streams

The Patriot (in sizes 14, 16, and 18) is often productive on small streams. The white wings of this attractor-type pattern show it well even under the heaviest canopies.

for six decades. He's caught fifteen-inch brown trout on streams less than ten feet wide. He's hooked native brookies on streams that contain only a trickle of water in late summer. Lloyd fly-fishes almost exclusively with attractor patterns. From his first trip to a stream in May until his last one in August, you'll find a Wulff Royal Coachman attached to his unusually heavy tippet. In fact, during much of the summer, the only time Lloyd changes the Royal Coachman off his line is when he ties on a new Coachman or tippet material.

What is an attractor pattern? What does it copy? An attractor doesn't copy any insect. Rather, the color is often so bizarre, so unusual, that it irritates trout into striking. Attractors often have bodies with yellow, red, blue, or some other unusual color.

Attractors work well on small streams. Many of them, like the Patriot and the Wulff Royal Coachman, have white upright wings which are easy to see in the half-light of a heavy canopy. White wings make these uprights much easier to follow than a terrestrial, even one with a fluorescent feather.

It's not necessary to carry many different patterns with you. You can rely on the two patterns I suggest and tie them in sizes 14, 16, and 18. Try the smaller sizes under low-water conditions in late summer.

Very little has been written about attractor downwings. Try tying the Patriot downwing (see Chapter 7). Tie the white wings so they lie back over the body or downwing. Native trout depend on caddis and stoneflies for much of their food supply. Doesn't it make sense to copy these two orders of insects with an attractor pattern that has downwings? On the several occasions that I've relied on a downwing Patriot, it performed well on mountain streams.

Streamers

Even though all the streams in the area were in flood stage, my brother, Jerry, still wanted to fly-fish for a half-day. Where could I take him? I decided on a small stream within twenty minutes of home. This stream almost never discolors in high water, and the level drops swiftly after a downpour.

When we arrived at the inundated stream, I knew only a small streamer would work. I tied on a small Woolly Bugger in a size 12 and worked my way downstream. Jerry tied on a small Lady Ghost streamer and headed downstream a half-mile below me. We agreed to fish for an hour, then to meet back at the car and compare notes on the fishing.

When we arrived back at the car, Jerry started telling me about the half-dozen heavy fish he had taken on the Lady Ghost streamer. That matched the number of trout I had caught on the Woolly Bugger. Both patterns worked well under these less-than-ideal conditions.

I often resort to streamers on small streams during the first few weeks of the season in spring and when I encounter high water throughout the season. Many streamers copy minnows and small trout. The Lady Ghost pattern effectively copies many of these smaller fish.

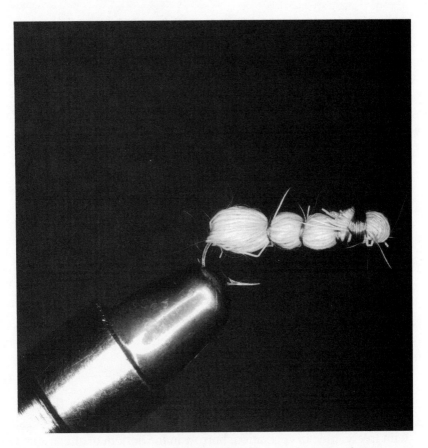

The Green Inchworm works extremely well on small streams during May, June, and July.

I've added the Green Weenie, Green Worm, and Green Inchworm to this group of patterns. Many would place this productive pattern with the terrestrials. This pattern copies many of the green inchworms you'll see during the summer. But I often add weight to the hook before I tie the pattern to make it sink to the bottom. Tie some in sinking and floating patterns. These work well all year long.

One day George Harvey and I met another fly-fisherman on one of our favorite small streams. The angler bragged about catching his limit each trip to the stream the past couple of weeks. All he ever used was a Green Weenie. He used this pattern consistently with unbelievable results. It's not the first time I met someone using this same fly and achieving terrific results.

The following are some streamers you should carry with you:

Woolly Bugger

Lady Ghost

Honey Bug

Green Weenie or Green Worm

Muddler Minnow

You will find the tying descriptions for some of the streamers in Chapter 7.

Patterns to Match the Hatches

In Chapter 6 you found information on matching the hatches on small streams. When a hatch appears, throw away your terrestrial, attractor, or other pattern, and copy the hatch. During the hatch native trout lose some of their timidity and go on a feeding rampage. When native trout feed on a hatch, they often move a considerable distance to take your pattern.

Nymphs

The immature stages of mayflies, stoneflies, and caddis flies are available to trout 365 days a year. These juvenile stages cling to rocks, swim freely, hide in vegetation, burrow in the bottom of streams and rivers, or build a protective shelter. Since trout see and feed on nymphs or larvae almost every day of the year, imitations of this stage should work successfully. They do!

Several years ago, at the Capitol Chapter of Trout Unlimited, someone asked why fly-fishermen meticulously match mayfly duns and spinners but seldom copy mayfly nymphs as closely. Adult mayflies, stoneflies, and caddis flies are available to trout for a week or less. Trout key in on the color, shape, and size of these adults for the short period that they're above water. Nymphs, on the other hand, appear as trout food every day of the year and in a myriad of colors. Examine any of your favorite streams and rivers and you'll see that these immature aquatic insects come in tan, gray, brown, yellow, and black.

Dan Shields is an outstanding nymph-fisherman who often conducts seminars on the techniques of nymph-fishing. You'll find him catching trout on Spring Creek on one of his nymph patterns. Follow him to one of his favorite small streams where you'll see him often use dry flies. On occasion, however, when those small streams become frustrating, he relies on nymphs to take trout.

Nymphs of dark brown, black, and gray catch trout on small streams. If you prefer using a nymph, make certain you tie on a short leader. A short 6- to 7-foot leader makes it easier to set the hook under close cover. The following are some of the patterns you should carry with you on small streams:

March Brown Nymph
Green Drake Nymph
Sulphur Nymph
Green Stonefly Nymph
Yellow Stonefly Nymph
Hare's Ear Nymph
Muskrat Nymph

Directions for creating many of these and others are found in the next chapter along with the duns and spinners of mayflies.

Wet Flies

Wet flies imitate emerging caddis and drowned mayfly adults and often catch trout when dry flies fail.

As a youngster, fishing one of my first small streams, I found wet flies saved me from total frustration on many days. At that time I had only two wet-fly patterns in my inventory. One of these was a dark brown wet fly listed as a March Brown on the package and the other a pale yellow wet fly tagged a Yellow Sally. Both caught dozens of trout for me and encouraged me to continue fly-fishing.

Wet flies like the March Brown, Light Cahill, and Leadwing Coachman work well on small trout streams. They work especially well in high water. Carry some wet-fly patterns like the following with you:

Light Cahill
March Brown
Leadwing Coachman
Cress Bug

The Green Drake imitation works well near the end of May on those small streams harboring a population of this large mayfly.

General Rules

Here are some general rules for selecting patterns on small water. When there's a hatch in progress, like a Green Drake, match the hatch with a dry fly, wet fly, or nymph of the species appearing. Try to match the size of the natural as closely as possible. If trout refuse a copy of the dry fly, switch to a wet fly or nymph.

If the water is extremely high, use a large wet fly, nymph, or streamer. Under low-water, late-summer conditions, resort as much as possible to dry flies, the smaller the better. Carry dry flies in sizes 14 to 18.

In July and August you'll find that terrestrials like ants and beetles work well. If the small stream you're fishing flows through an open field, you might consider using a grasshopper.

Remember, before you decide on the pattern you'll use on small streams, you must consider several factors. First, you'll often fly-fish under a heavy canopy with little sunlight hitting the water. If you've decided on a dry fly, make certain the pattern you select is large enough or bright enough to see. Use George Harvey's suggestion and tie your terrestrial patterns for those small streams with a fluorescent orange or red feather or tag on top. You'll be able to follow the pattern much more closely.

But you say you want to use an upright dry fly, not a terrestrial. Then use the attractors suggested or patterns like the Light Cahill under poor light conditions so you can detect them more easily.

All the patterns listed in this chapter work on small streams. The two categories of patterns that catch trout trip after trip on small streams are the attractors and the terrestrials. Give me an ant, beetle, Wulff Coachman, or a Patriot, and I can catch trout the majority of times. Don't head out to your favorite small creek without a generous supply of these last four patterns.

Remember, on most small streams, a dry fly will bring a trout to the surface.

7.
Tying the Patterns
for Small-Stream Fishing

YOU'LL SEE DIRECTIONS for tying some small-stream patterns on the following pages. But before you tie the patterns, look at the discussion of the main parts of a fly: wings, hackle, body, tail, and the hook.

Wings

George Harvey often uses hen hackle for wings on his dry flies. Bucky Metz, developer of Metz necks, recently gave George some new hen saddle hackle. George noticed that the hackle from these new saddles appeared much narrower than the former ones. George found that wings tied from these new necks didn't twist the leader. He used no wing-burner but tied them directly from the neck to the hook. (A wing-burner looks like a tweezer with the tip shaped like insect wings. After you place hen hackle in the wing-burner, you burn off the part of the feather protruding.) George now ties most of his size-10 to -16 dry flies with these exciting novel necks. George wrote an article on these new wings for *Fly Fisherman* magazine.

I use poly yarn to tie many of my small-stream dry-fly patterns. Use white poly or another color called for in making the wings, and tie them upright. These wings hold up well and help the pattern float. They're virtually indestructible. I rely almost exclusively on hen hackle or poly yarn to tie wings on all my flies. Years ago I used nothing but mallard quill sections to copy all gray wings. Many fly-tiers have difficulty tying quill sections. Also, mallard quills twist many of the newer, more supple, leaders.

Tails

Since you'll often get little chance to false cast a dry fly under a dense canopy, it's important to use a stiff tail to float any dry fly. Consider using deer hair or moose mane rather than rooster hackle fibers to make the tail more durable and buoyant.

Jim Bashline is an excellent fly-fisherman. He's written several books on fly-fishing and is an associate editor of *Field and Stream.* Jim prefers not to tie tails made of stiff hair. He theorizes that trout feel that part of the imitation first when they strike. He believes that they sense a tail made of hair much more quickly than one of hackle fibers and reject the fly by striking short.

Hackle

I can remember the first couple of necks I purchased from Herter's, a former mail order sporting goods company, when I first began tying flies. One neck, called a "bronze grizzly," contained dark gray grizzly hackle. Very few of these hackle, however, could be used for anything smaller than a size-14 pattern. The neck had virtually no size-16 or small hackle. Furthermore, the hackle were quite soft and did a poor job of floating the dry fly. Recent rooster necks like those sold by Bucky Metz have much stiffer barbules and do a much better job of floating the fly. On their Grade A necks you can easily get hackle for size-22 and -24 dry flies. Often one Metz hackle floats the fly adequately.

If false casting is at a premium on the small stream you plan to fly-fish, use two stiff hackle. The dry fly will float better with less time spent false casting.

Body

"Take a look at my Red Quill," Bob Bachman said. The body had become unraveled from the bend of the hook. Bob had just forced the fly out of a nearby bush on this small mountain stream. The brownish red hackle stem breaks easily. Just a few minutes earlier I had replaced a Quill Gordon that had split its peacock-herl body.

"No more of these," I said, "I'm going to rely on poly bodies from here on."

That happened several years ago. I now almost exclusively use poly for dry flies on small streams because it is buoyant, durable, and comes in a myriad of colors. To use many of the following patterns as wet flies, exchange the poly body for one of wool, fur, or other less buoyant material.

If you insist on patterns with quill bodies, you can do a couple of things to protect them from unraveling. Place a very fine gold wire over the body, or coat the body with a fine layer of tying cement.

Hooks

If you tie some of the streamers, terrestrials, attractors, nymphs, and wet flies I recommend, then you should have a general idea what hook should be used with what fly on small streams. But there are so many hooks available that it's difficult to keep abreast of all of them. Several years ago Dave Hughes presented a concise description of the various uses of the different hooks in an article in *Flyfishing*. Others have been added to his list. The numbers in table 7 refer to Mustad hooks. If your local supplier doesn't stock Mustad hooks, he'll be able to translate the numbers to those of the hooks he carries.

Problems have recently cropped up with the points on some of the better brands of hooks. You might buy a whole box of defective hooks so check with your dealer and examine at random some of the points before you purchase.

Dick Stewart's *The Hook Book* (Northland Press, Intervale, NH, 1986) covers Eagle Claw, Kamasan, Mustad, Partridge, Tiemco, and VMC hooks. For each hook the author includes diagrams, uses, possible substitutions, and vital statistics. This fine book is a must for all fly-tiers.

Table 7: Mustad Hooks and Their Function

Hook Number	Wire	Length	Purpose
Dry Fly			
94845	1x Fine	Standard	Dry fly, barbless
94842	1x Fine	Standard	Dry fly, turned-up eye
94840	1x Fine	Standard	Standard dry fly
94833	3x Fine	Standard	Light dry fly
94831	2x Fine	2XL	Used for large patterns like the Green Drake
Wet Fly			
3906	1x Stout	Standard	Standard wet fly
9671	1x Stout	2XL	Long wet fly
3908	2x Stout	Standard	Heavy wet fly
Nymphs			
3906B	1x Stout	1XL	Standard nymph hook
9672	1x Stout	3XL	Long nymphs and small streamers
37160*	1x Stout	Standard	Caddis larvae
Streamers			
9672	Standard	3XL	Small streamer
79580	Standard	4XL	Medium streamer
3665A	Standard	6XL	Large streamer
94720	Standard	8XL	Extra-large streamer

* Hook size is larger than normal

"Wire" in the hook table refers to the weight or strength of the hook. There are essentially three weights: fine, standard, and stout. A 2X fine hook contains the same wire found in a hook two sizes smaller. A Mustad hook 94831 in size 12 contains the same wire as a standard size-16 hook. Conversely, a stout wire rating indicates that the hook is heavier than normal. For instance, a size-12 hook in model 3908 is 2X stout. This hook has the same wire as a size-8 standard. Hooks with fine wire float better but have less strength than standard or stout hooks.

Hook lengths vary from short to standard to extra large. Remember, only the length of the shank is reduced as length decreases, not the gap (the distance between the point and the shank). Look at an extra-large size-12 hook, Mustad 9671 (2XL). This hook contains the same gap as a standard size-12 hook but has the length of a standard size-8 hook.

Mustad 37160 hooks are often used for tying emerging caddis pupa patterns. Check the size when ordering this hook. A size 14 appears as large as a size 10 in 3906.

Note in the chart that Mustad 94845 hooks are barbless. Barbless are usually more expensive than barbed hooks. Make your hooks barbless before you start tying; then if the point breaks before you tie, you can throw them away. Always use barbless hooks when tying flies for small-stream fly-fishing. Many of the native trout you'll catch hit so ferociously that the fly lodges deep within their mouths. Carry a hemostat with you so you can gently release all those fish that have taken the fly deep.

Tie some of your streamer patterns for small streams on 9672 hooks. This hook works well with the Muddler Minnow and the Lady Ghost. You'll see how to tie these patterns next.

Streamers

You'll find that many streamer and bucktail bodies contain silver or gold tinsel. When you use tinsel for the body, start at the eye, wind the tinsel back to the bend of the hook, then back to the front. Wrapping the shank twice covers any gap a single wrap would allow. Place a drop of cement over the wound tinsel.

I mentioned bucktails in the last paragraph. How do they differ from streamers? Both usually imitate minnows or baitfish, but a bucktail is a hair-winged fly, whereas a streamer is one constructed mainly of feathers. Both can be effective patterns on small streams, especially when you're faced with high water.

The following are some tying directions for streamer patterns:

Woolly Bugger
Thread: Black
Tail: A small handful of black marabou
Body: First, tie in a long black saddle hackle at the tail; size the

hackle for the hook you're using. Tie in a small piece of dark olive chenille at the hackle. Wind the chenille around the bend of the hook to the eye. Next, take the saddle hackle and palmer it over the chenille ending up at the eye. Cut off excess.
Hook: Mustad 9672, size 12 and 14

Lady Ghost
Thread: Black
Tail: None
Body: Flat silver tinsel, ribbed with silver oval tinsel
Throat: Five to ten white bucktail fibers tied on top of the same number of yellow bucktail fibers.
Wing: Four peacock herl placed under four long matched badger hackle. Match the hackle with two on each side. Have the tips of the hackle extend slightly past the bend of the hook.
Shoulder: Take a bright maroon feather from the neck of a ringneck pheasant. Tie one in on either side of the streamer.
Hook: Mustad 79580 or 9672, size 12 or 14

Terrestrials

Often when George Harvey and I fly-fished the same small stream together, he'd tie on a Deer-Hair Ant while I frequently started with an attractor pattern like the Patriot. Usually both of us did well with the two contrasting patterns. However, on a couple of occasions George caught two or three trout for every one I caught. On one small stream after I caught a couple of streambred brown trout with the pattern, I began to tie on a new pattern. The deer hair broke, and the ant lost its shape. I was about to discard the fly, but George asked me what I was doing and told me to keep that half-torn ant on. I did and I caught more trout. The hairier—the buggier—it looked, the more trout I caught.

You might want to consider tying your ant and beetle patterns from one of the new materials like polycelon. Ants and beetles tied from this float well. Again, as with all small terrestrial patterns, add a fluorescent feather, poly, or tag of some sort to help you locate the pattern on the water.

If you want to tie terrestrials with the least amount of effort, then you

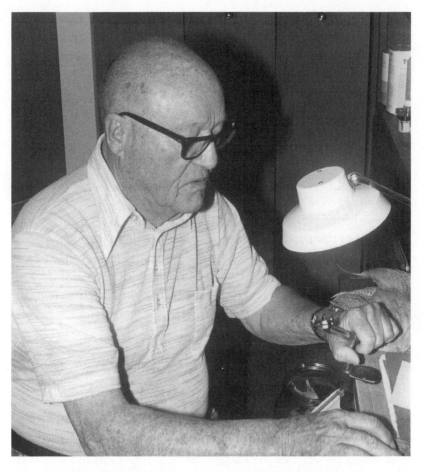

George Harvey tying up a terrestrial pattern to use on one of his favorite small streams.

want to tie the Poly Ant. It takes less than a minute to tie but is an effective pattern on small streams.

One of the best patterns for Deer-Hair Ants is the one listed in George Harvey's new book, *Techniques of Trout Fishing and Fly Tying*. This comprehensive book discloses George's method of tying this buggy-looking terrestrial. I said earlier that after you catch a few trout with one of these Deer-Hair Ants, the hairs begin to split. After catching a half-dozen or dozen native trout, the pattern looks like anything but an ant. Each of the broken hairs make another simulated leg.

Deer-Hair Ant

Body: Black deer hair

Hook: Sizes 12 to 18

Take a bunch of black deer hair about 1½ times as long as the shank of the hook. Tie in the butts at the middle of the shank with the tips pointing toward the bend of the hook. Move the thread to the bend, tie in the deer hair, and move the thread back to the center of the shank. Pull the deer-hair tip back over the butt and again tie in at the center of the shank. Pull remaining deer-hair tips to the eye and tie in. Make certain the two piles of deer hair form the two humps of an ant. Clip off excess hair at the eye. Pull out three hairs from the rear hump with a bodkin. These become the legs of the ant.

Poly Ant

Body: Black poly, dubbed into two humps on the hook with the rear hump being a bit larger than the front one.

Hackle: Add a black hackle after you complete the rear hump and before you start the front one.

Hook: Sizes 12 to 18

Essentially, you can substitute black poly for the deer hair, and you get the Poly Ant. This version lasts much longer than the Deer Hair Ant. You can dub the poly or use poly yarn.

After the ant, the beetle is my second choice of terrestrials on small streams. You can either tie the Poly Beetle or a Crowe Beetle. You tie the former with several strands of poly yarn and the latter with deer hair dyed black. Just as in the Deer-Hair Ant, the deer hair on the Crowe Beetle breaks quickly.

Poly Beetle

The Poly Beetle is tied exactly like the Crowe Beetle using black poly yarn rather than black deer hair. On a size-16 beetle use three strands of the yarn (about three match sticks thick). Tie in the poly securely below the bend of the hook. If you wish, tie in a peacock herl at the bend of the hook to imitate the Japanese Beetle. Wind the tying thread up to the eye of the hook and wind the peacock. Pull the poly up over the shank of the hook and tie in securely just behind the eye. Cut off the excess poly, but leave some to imitate the head. You'll really like this excellent pattern. It's simple, realistic, and takes less than a minute to tie. Tie on hook sizes 12 to 20.

LeTort Cricket

Body: Black poly, heavily dubbed
Wings: Black dyed goose quill sections, tied downwing
Hackle: Deer body hair, dyed black and tied in similar to the Muddler

On occasion the cricket can work well on small streams. I firmly believe larger patterns on low water scare trout. I rely on the cricket in the middle of summer only after a heavy downpour and when streams run higher than normal. Tie the cricket just as you'd normally tie a Muddler Minnow. With the cricket use black poly for the body, black deer hair for the legs, and add black goose quills on the side of the body.

Ken's Hopper

Body: Yellowish olive poly, dubbed heavily
Head and wings: Use deer body hair dyed yellow and tie in just behind the eye as you would with the muddler. Clip the butts also as in the Muddler.

Use the grasshopper on small streams with some open fields. Normally you won't see many grasshoppers in wooded areas; but when you fly-fish a small stream in an open area, give this terrestrial a try.

Green Weenie

To tie the Green Weenie, take a piece of fluorescent chartreuse chenille and tie it in at the bend of the hook. Make a small loop in the chenille about one fourth the length of the shank of the hook. The loop becomes the tail. Wind the remainder of the chenille around the shank of the hook up to the eye. Cut off the excess and tie in.

If you plan to use a floating inchworm, tie on a round-shaped cork cylinder. Use a razor blade and cut a slash lengthwise in the cork. Place the split part over the hook and press down. Tie the cork onto a

Mustad 94841, size 12 or 14. Paint the cork with a light bright green or chartreuse enamel.

You can also use deer body hair dyed chartreuse. Tie on the deer hair and clip to size.

Use the following pattern if you're tying the Green Inch Worm or Gypsy Moth.

Use bright green (black for the Gypsy Moth) elk or deer hair. Cut off a bunch of hair, the diameter of a pencil, and tie onto a size-12 or -14 hook (Mustad 94831) or other hook to match the size of the caterpillar. Make certain the hairs are at least three inches long. Tie the butts of the hair in tightly below the bend of the hook. Wind the thread forward one fifth of the way to the eye of the hook. Bring the hair forward, making certain that some of it is on the bottom, sides, and top of the hook. Make several winds just in front of the bunch of hair (this tends to make the hair thicker), then wind over the top of it, giving it a ribbed effect. Repeat this process four or five times until you reach the eye of the hook. Cut the excess tips off at the eye and whip finish.

Tying the Downwings

Always carry an ample supply of diverse patterns copying these important insects. Caddis imitations can mean the difference between a frustrating and a rewarding day. Include some caddis patterns with hackle. The hackled patterns are called "fluttering" caddis patterns by fly-fishermen. The fluttering caddis ride fast water higher than a second type, the Deer Head Caddis.

Include caddis with yellow, cream, tan, black, brown, and gray bodies in your supply.

Caddis patterns

The usual method for imitating wings on a caddis is to tie deer hair in by the butt just behind the eye of the hook. With this method of tying, the hair tends to roll, however, and it's difficult to achieve a smooth head on the imitation. Try tying, instead, a Deer Head Caddis. It is easier to tie, and the final product is a better copy of the natural. The end result resembles a smaller version of the Fulsher Minnow. To tie the Deer Head Caddis, follow these instructions:

Begin by tying in a bunch of cut deer hair, just as with the fluttering caddis. Place the deer hair so the butts are facing toward the rear (not the front) of the hook and the hair tips extend well out past the eye of the hook. Take your tying thread and wind it securely up over the deer-hair butts forward to the eye of the hook. Take a small piece of poly of the proper color, and dub it in just behind the eye. This little piece of dubbed poly becomes the chin of the caddis. Pull the tips of the deer hair back over the hook, and tie in about one fourth of the way back from the eye. Finish off with a whip finish, lacquer the head and thread, and you have a Deer-Head Caddis. If the wings of the natural caddis you want to imitate are darker than the deer hair, use moose mane or darker deer hair.

Green Caddis
Copies many members of the genus *Rhyacophila*.

Deer-Head Green Caddis
Thread: Brown
Body: Medium olive green poly with a gray cast, dubbed
Wings: Medium brown deer hair tied in with butts pointing toward the bend of the hook and the tips of the deer hair extending out over the eye of the hook. Tie in hair securely near the eye of the hook; then wind thread one fourth of the way back toward the bend. Bend deer hair back and tie in.
Hackle: If you prefer the regular fluttering caddis, you can tie as above and add a ginger hackle where you tie in the hair. Place a drop of lacquer on thread and finished head.
Hook: Mustad 94840, 37160, size 14 and 16

Spotted Sedge
Copies *Symphitopsyche slossanae*
Thread: Tan
Body: Grayish tan poly, dubbed
Wings: Medium brown deer hair
Hackle: Ginger
Hook: Mustad 94840, 37160, size 14 and 16

Dark Blue Sedge
  Copies *Psilotreta frontalis*
  Thread: Dark gray
  Body: Dark gray poly, dubbed
  Wings: Dark grayish brown deer hair
  Hackle: Dark brownish black
  Hook: Mustad 94840, 37160, size 12

Grannom
  Copies many species of the genus *Brachycentrus*
  Thread: Black
  Body: Dark brownish black to black poly, dubbed
  Wings: Dark brown deer hair
  Hackle: Dark brown
  Hook: Mustad 94840, 37160, size 12 and 14

Little Black Caddis
  Copies *Chimarra atterima*
  Thread: Black
  Body: Black poly, dubbed
  Wings: Deer hair dyed dark gray
  Hackle: Dark brown
  Hook: Mustad 94840, 37160, size 16

Caddis Larva
  Thread: Appropriate color (most often dark brown or black)
  Body: Olive, green, brown, yellow, black, or tan fur dubbed and ribbed with fine wire, or use a rubber band of the appropriate color and tie in at the bend of the hook and spiral to the eye.
  Thorax: Dark brown fur, dubbed; or an ostrich herl, dyed dark brown wound around the hook several times.
  Hook: Mustad 37160, size 12 to 18

Emerging Caddis Pupa
  Thread: Same color as the body color you select
  Body: Olive, green, brown, yellow, black, or tan fur or poly nymph dubbing material.

Wings: Dark mallard quill sections shorter than normal and tied in on both sides of the fly, not on top.

Legs: Dark brown grouse or woodcock neck feather wound around the hook two or three times.

Hook: Mustad 37160, size 12 to 18

Tying Mayfly Imitations

You'll often copy mayflies with four types of patterns—one copying the dun, another the spinner, one the nymph, and a wet fly to imitate drowned adults.

Tying Duns

Many new fly-tying methods and materials have come and gone since my *Meeting and Fishing the Hatches* (Winchester Press, New York, 1977) was published. In that book I recommended using mallard quill wing to imitate the dark gray wings so common on many emerging duns. These quill sections effectively copy the wings of all Blue Quill species, all of the Slate Drakes, the Quill Gordon, and all of the Olive Duns. When you use these wings on any pattern larger than a size 18, however, they tend to twist the new fine leader tippets. Dun hen hackle tips, shaped with a wing-burner, on the other hand, are much easier to tie and don't twist the line. Many of the Metz hen saddles now have hackle that don't need to be trimmed or burned.

I recommend using poly for body material on dry flies as much as possible. Today there are more varieties and colors of poly than ever before. Use the synthetic material in place of the natural quill bodies because the poly is much more durable. How many times has a Red Quill, Ginger Quill, or a Quill Gordon body unraveled after catching a few trout? This won't happen with poly. Use dark-gray poly for the body of Slate Drakes, light brown for the Ginger Quill, and reddish brown for the Red Quill.

I haven't discussed compara duns or methods for tying them. Although these patterns are extremely effective, they don't hold up as well as hackled flies. Check the compara duns you tied last year, and see how straight the wings are now.

Tying Spinner Imitations

Many female spinners die spent on the surface after laying their eggs. Others—Sulphur Spinners and Ginger Quills, for example—sometimes ride the water with their wings upright, just like the duns of the species. Conversely, male spinners of many species never get close to the water but meet the female, mate, and die over land. Knowing beforehand a mayfly's mating behavior helps when fishing the spinner fall. If you fly-fish small streams in the evening, then on occasion you'll encounter spinner falls.

Since many of the spinners ride the surface for some distance with wings upright and not spent, it's important to include some of these upright patterns in your selection. There's a bonus to using an upright spinner pattern—the imitation is much easier to follow on the surface than is a spent-wing, especially at dusk on small enclosed streams. The upright version of the Sulphur Spinner performs well in June and July on many eastern and midwestern branches and tributaries.

Orvis and other top companies supply a good poly yarn for spent-wings. Use this same material to tie the pattern upright, but tie the poly in as you would with calf tail and divide.

In many of my spinner patterns I include a few strands of Orvis Krystal Flash with the poly spent-wings. George Harvey first recommended using this material in an article on the Trico in *Fly Fisherman* magazine. Using a few strands of this material seems to produce more strikes.

Tying Wet Flies

Wet-fly patterns copying the Quill Gordon and other early hatches are deadly in April. One of the most memorable trips I've ever made was a day on the upper reaches of northeastern Pennsylvania's Mehoopany Creek. No dry fly or wet fly seemed to work that day until I switched to a Quill Gordon wet. There were a few Gordons in the air but no massive hatch. That didn't stop just about every trout in the particular pool from taking that wet fly.

Wet flies produce because they copy many emerging caddis and mayflies. They work exceptionally well in April and May and again in September and October.

The second hook number in the list of patterns later in this chapter refers to the wet-fly hook. Since in tying a wet fly you're tying a pattern you want to sink, use a less buoyant body material than poly. Fur, wool, and some other body materials sink quickly, and they come in an assortment of colors for any wet-fly pattern. Use hen hackle for the tail and legs, and dark mallard quill sections, hackle tips, and flank feathers for wings. Tie the wings parallel to the body.

Tying Nymphs

Nymphs are available as food for trout a good part of fishes' lives. It's essential, then, that you imitate nymphs on occasion. These patterns work well before and during a hatch when the naturals move toward the surface and begin emerging. You'll note in the tying directions that we suggest angora, opossum, or just plain fur as body material. All absorb water quickly and sink rapidly. Another material, called Ultra Translucent Nymph Dubbing, sold in many of the better fly-tying stores, is an excellent dubbing material for nymphs.

To make nymphs less buoyant, no matter what body material you use, you might want to incorporate some weight onto the body of the nymph. Just add a piece of lead wire and wind it around the hook to get the desired sinking action.

When we use the word "wings" in the tying descriptions for nymphs, we're really referring to the insects' wing pads; and when we list "hackle" in the instructions, we're referring to the legs of the insect. Tie in the wings about halfway back on the shank of the hook. Wind the tying thread over the tip of the wing section with the shiny side of the wing up and the butt of the section pointing back toward the bend of the hook. Leave the wing pad in that position until you've completed dubbing the front end of the body and have tied in the legs or hackle. Next, take the proper soft hackle and tie it in at the same place you tied in the wing pad. Finish dubbing the front part of the body; then wind the hackle over that. Trim the top part of the hackle; bring the wing pad up over the hackle; and tie it in at the eye.

You'll note that we recommend using cree or ginger-variant hackle quite often to copy the legs of nymphs and duns. Ginger-variant hackle normally includes dark and light brown shading on the same hackle, and cree contains cream, black, and brown barring. Both duplicate the multicolored legs of naturals quite well. The cream variant provides a lighter hackle than the ginger variant.

Tying Descriptions

Attractor patterns

Patriot
  Wing: White calf tail or impala
  Tail: Brown hackle fibers
  Body: Midsection is red floss; smolt blue Krystal Flash is on either side of the floss
  Hackle: Brown
  Hook: Mustad 94840, size 14

Wulff Royal Coachman
  Wing: White impala
  Tail: White impala
  Body: Midsection of red floss, with peacock on either side
  Hackle: Brown
  Hook: Mustad 94840, size 14

Remember if you want to tie some downwing versions of these two effective attractors, add the wings last and tie them back over the body. If you have difficulty following patterns on those heavily canopied small brooks, then keep the wings white but tie them down over the body.

Patterns for eastern and midwestern small-stream hatches

Blue Dun or Little Blue-Winged Olive Dun
  Copies *Baetis tricaudatus* and some *Pseudocloeon* species.
  Thread: Dark gray
  Tail: Medium to dark gray hackle fibers
  Body: Gray muskrat or medium gray poly, dubbed; for the Little Blue-Winged Olive use olive gray poly.

Wings: On smaller sizes (20) use dark gray mallard quills; on larger
sizes use dark gray hackle tips.
Hackle: Blue dun
Hook: Mustad 94840, 3906, sizes 18 and 20

Rusty Spinner
Thread: Dark brown
Tail: Dark grayish brown hackle fibers
Body: Grayish brown poly, dubbed and ribbed with fine tan thread
Wings: Pale gray poly yarn, tied spent
Hook: Same as above

Nymph
Thread: Dark olive
Tail: Wood duck fibers, dyed dark olive
Body: Dark olive brown opossum
Wings: Dark gray mallard quill section
Hackle: Cree or ginger-variant hackle, dyed dark olive
Hook: 3906B, size 18

Blue Quill
Copies all *Paraleptophlebia* species.
Thread: Dark gray
Tail: Medium to dark gray hackle fibers
Body: Eyed peacock herl, stripped or dark gray poly, dubbed
Wings: Dark gray hackle tips
Hackle: Light to medium blue dun
Hook: Mustad 94840, 3906, size 18 or 20

Dark-Brown Spinner
Thread: Dark brown
Tail: Dark brown hackle fibers
Body: Dark brown poly, dubbed
Wings: Pale gray poly yarn, tied spent
Hook: Same as above

Nymph
Thread: Dark Brown
Tail: Mallard flank feather, dyed dark brown

The Blue-Winged Olive Dun works well on small streams in late May and early June.

Body: Dark brown angora, dubbed
Wings: One dark gray mallard quill tied down
Hackle: Dark gray
Hook: 3906B, size 16 and 18

Blue-Winged Olive Dun
Copies many *Drunella (Ephemerella)* species and *Dannella (Ephemerella)* like *cornuta, longicornus.*
Thread: Olive
Tail: Grayish olive hackle fibers
Body: Light to medium olive poly, dubbed
Wings: Dark gray hackle tips
Hackle: Medium creamish olive
Hook: Mustad 94840, 3906, size 14 to 20

Dark-Olive Spinner
Thread: Dark olive or black
Tail: Moose mane (dark brown)
Body: Dark olive poly (almost black with an olive cast)
Wings: Pale gray poly yarn, tied spent
Hook: Same as above

Nymph
  Thread: Olive
  Tail: Wood duck
  Body: Dark brown angora tied over dubbed-in olive opossum
  Wings: Brown turkey
  Hackle: Ginger variant, dyed olive
  Hook: 3906B, sizes 14 to 18

Quill Gordon
  Copies species like *Epeorus pleuralis.*
  Thread: Dark gray
  Tail: Dark gray hackle fibers
  Body: Eyed peacock herl, stripped and lacquered
  Wings: Wood duck or imitation wood duck, divided; or dark gray
    hackle tips
  Hackle: Dark gray hackle
  Hook: Mustad 94840, 3906, size 14
Red Quill Spinner
  Use same pattern as spinner listed under Hendrickson.

Nymph
  Thread: Dark brown
  Tail: Fibers from a mallard flank feather, dyed dark amber
  Body: Dark brown fur or angora, mixed with a bit of lighter brown
    or amber
  Wings: Mottled brown turkey, tied down over thorax
  Hackle: Cree or ginger-variant hackle (dark and amber mixed)
  Hook: 3906B, size 14

Light Cahill
  Copies *Stenacron interpunctatum* subspecies which is sometimes
    found on small streams.
  Thread: Cream or tan
  Tail: Cream hackle fibers
  Body: Cream poly, fox fur, or angora, dubbed
  Wings: Mallard flank feather, dyed pale yellow, divided
  Hackle: Cream hackle
  Hook: Mustad 94840, 3906, size 14

Light Cahill Spinner
    Same as dun except omit hackle and add pale yellow poly yarn for
    wings. Tie them spent.

Nymph
    Thread: Brown
    Tail: Fibers from a mallard flank feather, dyed brown
    Body: Dark brown angora yarn on top and pale amber belly, dubbed
    Wings: Dark brown turkey
    Hackle: Dark cree
    Hook: 3906B, size 12

Slate Drake
    Copies many *Isonychia* species which frequent small streams.
    Thread: Black
    Tail: Dark gray hackle fibers
    Body: Peacock herl (not from eye), stripped; or dark gray poly, or
    muskrat, dubbed
    Wings: Dark gray hackle tips
    Hackle: One cream hackle tied in behind and one dark brown hackle
    tied in front
    Hook: Mustad 94840, 3906, size 12 or 14

White-Gloved Howdy
    Thread: Dark brown or maroon
    Tail: Medium gray hackle fibers
    Body: Dark mahogany poly, dubbed
    Wings: Pale gray poly yarn
    Hook: Same as above

Nymph
    Thread: Dark brown
    Tail: Three dark brown hackle with one side cut off
    Body: Very dark brown angora or opossum
    Wings: Dark gray mallard quill section, tied down over thorax
    Hackle: Cree hackle, dyed pale olive
    Hook: 3906B, size 10 or 12

Sulphur Dun

Copies *Ephemerella rotunda, invaria, septentrionalis,* and, to a lesser degree, *dorothea.* All can be found on small streams.

Thread: Yellow

Tail: Cream hackle fibers

Body: Usually pale yellow poly with an orange (and sometimes olive orange) cast

Wings: Pale gray hackle tips

Hackle: Cream hackle

Hook: Mustad 94840, 3906, size 16 and 18

Sulphur Spinner

Thread: Tan

Tail: Tan deer hair

Body: Female with eggs—yellowish tan poly; female without eggs—tan poly; male—bright red hackle stem, stripped and wound around hook

Wings: Pale gray poly yarn, tied spent (also tie some upright)

Hook: Same as above

Nymph

Thread: Grayish brown

Tail: Brown pheasant tail fibers

Body: Brown (ground color) fur

Wings: Dark gray mallard quill section, tied down over thorax

Hackle: Cree hackle

Hook: 3906B, size 14, 16, and 18

Red Quill and Hendrickson

Red Quill copies the male and the Hendrickson the female of *Ephemerella subvaria* and several closely related subspecies. In addition, the Red Quill effectively imitates many spinners like *Ephemerella subvaria, Epeorus pleuralis,* and the male spinner of *Ephemerella invaria* and *rotunda.*

Thread: Brown

Tail: Medium gray hackle fibers

Body: Red Quill—reddish brown hackle fiber stripped of its barbules

and wound from the bend of the hook to the wings. Hendrickson—
tan poly, dubbed.

Wings: Wood duck, divided. Optional on Hendrickson are gray
hackle tips.

Hackle: Medium gray hackle

Hook: Mustad 94840, 3906, sizes 14 and 16

Red Quill Spinner

Thread: Brown

Tail: Bronze dun hackle fibers

Body: Dark tannish brown poly, dubbed and ribbed finely with tan
thread

Wings: Pale gray poly yarn, tied spent

Hook: Same as above

Nymph

Thread: Dark brown

Tail: Fibers from a mallard flank feather, dyed brown

Body: Dark brown angora, mixed with a bit of amber

Wings: Mottled brown turkey, tied down over thorax

Hackle: Cree hackle

Hook: 3906B, size 12 and 14

Green Drake

Copies *Ephemera guttulata.*

Thread: Cream

Tail: Moose mane

Body: Cream poly, dubbed

Wings: Mallard flank dyed yellowish green, divided

Hackle: Rear—cream hackle; front—dark brown hackle

Hook: Mustad 94831, 3906B, sizes 8 and 10

Coffin Fly

Thread: White

Tail: Light tan deer hair

Body: White poly, dubbed

Wings: Grayish yellow poly yarn, tied spent

Hook: Same as above

Nymph
  Thread: Tan
  Tail: Three medium brown hackle, trimmed and tied in
  Body: Pale tan angora
  Wings: Dark brown turkey, tied down and over thorax
  Hackle: Cree
  Hook: 3906B, or 9672, size 8 to 12

March Brown
  Copies *Stenonema vicarium.*
  Thread: Yellow
  Tail: Dark brown hackle fibers
  Body: Tan poly, dubbed and ribbed with dark brown thread
  Wings: Mallard flank feather, dyed yellowish brown and divided
  Hackle: One cream and one dark brown, mixed
  Hook: Mustad 94840, 3906, size 12

Great Red Spinner
  Thread: Dark brown
  Tail: Dark brown hackle fibers
  Body: Dark reddish brown poly, dubbed
  Wings: Pale gray poly yarn, tied spent
  Hackle: Dark brown with a turn or two of pale ginger mixed
  Hook: Same as above

Nymph
  Thread: Brown
  Tail: Fibers from a mallard flank feather, dyed brown
  Body: Same as Gray Fox below
  Wings: Dark brown turkey, tied down over thorax
  Hackle: Dark cree
  Hook: 3906B, size 12

Gray Fox
  Copies *Stenonema fuscum.*
  Thread: Cream
  Tail: Tan deer hair
  Body: Cream poly, dubbed
  Wings: Mallard flank feather, dyed pale yellowish tan, divided

Hackle: Cree hackle or one brown and one cream mixed
Hook: Mustad 94840, 3906, size 12 or 14

Ginger Quill Spinner
  Thread: Brown
  Tail: Dark brown hackle fibers
  Body: Eyed peacock herl, dyed tan and stripped, or grayish brown
    poly, ribbed with brown thread
  Wings: Gray hackle tips (conventional); or pale gray poly yarn, tied
    spent
  Hackle: Dark ginger (conventional); or none with poly yarn wings
  Hook: Same as above

Nymph
  Thread: Brown
  Tail: Fibers from a mallard flank feather, dyed brown
  Body: Brown angora yarn, tied on top over cream. Tie in brown at
    tail, and dub in cream so that top *(tergites)* of body is brown and
    the belly *(sternites)* is cream.
  Wings: Dark brown turkey, tied down over thorax
  Hackle: Dark cree
  Hook: 3906B, size 12

Chocolate Dun
  Copies species like *Eurylophella (Ephemerella) bicolor.*
  Thread: Brown
  Tail: Medium gray
  Body: Chocolate brown poly finely ribbed with lighter brown
    thread
  Wings: Dark gray hackle tips
  Hackle: Tan hackle
  Hook: Mustad 94840, 3906, size 16

Chocolate Spinner
  Thread: Dark brown
  Tail: Tannish gray hackle fibers
  Body: Dark rusty brown poly, dubbed
  Wings: Pale gray poly yarn, tied spent
  Hook: Same as above

If you arrive early at a small stream that has a hatch of Tricos, you might see trout rising to the female dun. This imitation of the Trico Dun works well.

Dark Green Drake
Copies small-stream species like *Litobrancha recurvata*.
Thread: Dark gray
Tail: Dark brown moose mane
Body: Very dark slate poly, dubbed and ribbed with yellow thread
Wings: Mallard flank, heavily barred and dyed dark green
Hackle: Rear—tannish brown hackle; front—dark brown hackle
Hook: Mustad 94833, 3906B, size 8 or 10

Brown Drake Spinner
Thread: Brown
Tail: Brown hackle fibers
Body: Reddish brown poly, dubbed and ribbed with yellow thread
Wings: Pale gray poly yarn, tied spent
Hackle: Dark brown
Hook: Same as above

Nymph
Thread: Light brown
Tail: Three dark bronze hackles, trimmed and tied in

Body: Tan with a grayish cast angora, or opossum
Wings: Dark brown turkey
Hackle: Dark cree
Hook: 9672, size 8 or 10

Trico
Copies all *Tricorythodes* species.

Dun
Thread: Pale olive
Tail: Cream hackle fibers
Body: Pale olive green poly, dubbed; male dun—dark brown poly
Wings: Pale gray hackle tips
Hackle: Cream hackle
Hook: Mustad 94840, size 20 to 24

Trico Spinner
Thread: Dark brown
Tail: Female—short cream hackle fibers; male—long dark brown moose mane
Body: Female—rear one third is cream poly, dubbed, and front two-thirds is dark brown poly, dubbed; male—dark brown poly, dubbed and ribbed with a very fine light tan thread
Wings: White poly yarn, tied spent
Hook: Mustad 94840, size 20 to 24

Nymph
Thread: Black
Tail: Dark brown hackle fibers
Body: Dark brownish black fur
Wings: Dark gray mallard quill section
Hackle: Dark reddish brown
Hook: 3906B, size 22

Pale Evening Dun
Copies species like *Ephemerella dorothea, E. septentrionalis* and many *Heptagenia* species like *H. walshi, aphrodite,* and others. *Ephemerella dorothea* is especially important on small streams.
Thread: Pale yellow

If you find a small stream with a Trico hatch and match the hatch, you can have several months of fly-fishing enjoyment each season.

Tail: Cream hackle fibers
Body: Pale yellowish cream poly, dubbed
Wings: Pale yellow hackle tips
Hackle: Cream
Hook: Mustad 94840, 3906, size 16 to 20

Pale Evening Spinner
  Thread: Cream
  Tail: Cream hackle fibers
  Body: Pale yellowish cream poly, dubbed
  Wings: Pale gray poly yarn, tied spent
  Hook: Same as above

Nymph
  Thread: Brown
  Tail: Dark brown pheasant tail fibers
  Body: Dark tan ultra translucent dubbing
  Wings: Gray mallard quill section
  Hackle: Cree
  Hook: Mustad 3906B, size 16 and 18

Patterns for western hatches found on small streams

Western March Brown
Copies *Rhithrogena morrisoni* and *hageni.*
Thread: Brown
Tail: Medium brown
Body: Medium brown poly, dubbed
Wings: Medium gray hackle wings
Hackle: Dark brown hackle
Hook: 94840, 3906, size 14

Dark Tan Spinner
Thread: Tan
Tail: Dark brown hackle fibers
Body: Dark brown poly, dubbed
Wings: Pale gray poly yarn
Hook: 94840, 3906, size 14

Nymph
Thread: Dark brown
Tail: Imitation wood duck fibers
Body: Dark reddish brown fur
Wings: Dark brown turkey
Hackle: Very dark cree hackle
Hook: 3903B, size 14

Blue Quill
Copies all small-water *Paraleptophlebia* species including *debilis, heteronea, memorialis, gregalis,* and *bicornuta.*
Thread: Dark gray
Tail: Medium gray hackle fibers
Body: Eyed peacock herl, stripped
Wings: Dark gray hackle tips
Hackle: Medium gray or dun
Hook: Mustad 94840, 3906, size 18

Dark Brown Spinner
Thread: Dark brown

Tail: Dark brown hackle fibers
Body: Dark brown poly, dubbed
Wings: Pale gray poly yarn, tied spent
Hook: Same as above

Nymph
    Thread: Dark brown
    Tail: Mallard flank feather, dyed dark brown
    Body: Dark brown angora, dubbed
    Wings: One dark gray mallard quill
    Hackle: Dark gray
    Hook: 3906B, size 16 and 18

Blue Dun or Little Blue-Winged Olive Dun
    Copies *Baetis bicaudatus, tricaudatus, intermedius,* and others and
      some *Pseudocloeon* species.
    Thread: Dark gray
    Tail: Medium to dark gray hackle fibers
    Body: Gray muskrat or medium gray poly with a slight olive cast,
      dubbed (the body of *Baetis bicaudatus* is more olive than the
      others).
    Wings: On smaller sizes (20) use dark gray mallard quills; on larger
      sizes use dark gray hackle tips.
    Hackle: Blue Dun
    Hook: Mustad 94840, 3906, size 18 and 20

Rusty Spinner
    Thread: Dark brown
    Tail: Dark grayish brown hackle fibers
    Body: Grayish brown poly, dubbed and ribbed with fine tan thread
    Wings: Pale gray poly yarn, tied spent
    Hook: Mustad 94840, size 18 and 20

Nymph
    Thread: Dark olive
    Tail: Wood duck fibers, dyed dark olive
    Body: Dark olive brown opossum
    Wings: Dark gray mallard quill section

Hackle: Cree hackle, dyed dark olive
Hook: 3906B, size 18

Trico
Copies all *Tricorythodes* species.
Thread: Pale olive
Tail: Cream hackle fibers
Body: Pale olive poly, dubbed
Wings: Pale gray hackle tips
Hackle: Cream hackle
Hook: Mustad 94840, 3906 size 20 to 24

Trico Spinner
Thread: Dark brown
Tail: Female—short cream hackle fibers; male—long dark brown moose mane
Body: Female—rear one third is cream poly, dubbed, and front two thirds is dark brown poly, dubbed; male—dark brown poly, dubbed and ribbed with a very fine light tan thread
Wings: White poly yarn, tied spent
Hook: Mustad 94840, size 20 to 24

Nymph
Thread: Black
Tail: Dark brown hackle fibers
Body: Dark brownish black fur
Wings: Dark gray mallard quill section
Hackle: Dark reddish brown
Hook: 3906B, size 22

Blue-Winged Olive Dun
Copies *Drunella flavilinea.*
Thread: Olive
Tail: Grayish olive hackle fibers
Body: Light to medium olive poly, dubbed
Wings: Dark gray hackle tips
Hackle: Medium creamish olive
Hook: Mustad 94840, 3906, size 14 to 20

Dark Olive Spinner
  Thread: Dark olive or black
  Tail: Moose mane (dark brown)
  Body: Dark olive poly (almost black with an olive cast)
  Wings: Pale gray poly yarn, tied spent
  Hook: Same as above

Nymph
  Thread: Olive
  Tail: Wood duck
  Body: Dark brown angora tied over dubbed-in olive opossum
  Wings: Brown turkey
  Hackle: Cree, dyed olive
  Hook: 3906B, sizes 14 to 18

Pale Evening Dun
  Copies species like *Heptagenia elegantula.*
  Thread: Pale yellow
  Tail: Cream hackle fibers
  Body: Pale yellowish cream poly, dubbed
  Wings: Pale yellow hackle tips
  Hackle: Cream
  Hook: Mustad 94840, 3906, size 16 to 20

Pale Evening Spinner
  Thread: Cream
  Tail: Cream hackle fibers
  Body: Pale yellowish cream poly, dubbed
  Wings: Pale gray poly yarn, tied spent
  Hook: Same as above

Pale Morning Dun
  Copies species like *Ephemerella inermis* and *Ephemerella infre-quens.* Both are common on small streams.
  Thread: Cream
  Tail: Cream hackle fibers
  Body: Varies from a bright olive to a creamish yellow. Use poly and dub.

Wings: Very pale gray hackle tips
Hackle: Cream
Hook: Mustad 94840, 3906, size 16 and 18

Pale Morning Spinner
  Thread: Orange
  Tail: Tan
  Body: Tan
  Wings: Pale gray poly yarn
  Hooks: Mustad 94840, size 16 and 18

Nymph
  Thread: Dark brown
  Tail: Mallard flank fibers, dyed ginger
  Body: Belly is amber angora or nymph dubbing with a darker brown
    back
  Wings: Brown turkey
  Hackle: Cree
  Hook: 39060, size 16 or 18

Stoneflies

Acroneuria Nymph
  Thread: Dark brown
  Tail: Light brown hackle fibers
  Body: Dark olive brown yarn, laid over top of pale yellow dubbing
    fur
  Wings: Dark brown turkey
  Hackle: Cree
  Hook: 3906B, size 10 and 12

Little Green Stonefly
  Copies small-stream species like *Alloperla imbecilla.*
  Thread: Green
  Tail: Short pale cream hackle fibers
  Body: Medium green poly, dubbed
  Wings: pale gray hackle tips, tied downwing
  Hackle: Pale creamish green hackle
  Hook: Mustad 94840, size 16

Nymph
Thread: Yellow
Tail: Pale yellow
Body: Use poly that is pale yellow with a hint of olive
Wing case: Pale yellowish olive mallard flank
Hackle: Pale yellow hackle
Hook: Mustad 3906B, size 16

Yellow Stonefly
Copies species like *Isoperla bilineata.*
Thread: Yellow
Tail: Short cream hackle fibers
Body: Pale yellow poly, dubbed
Wings: Cream hackle tips, tied downwing
Hackle: Cree hackle
Hook: Mustad 94840, size 14 or 16

Nymph
Thread: Pale yellow
Tail: Pale yellow hackle fibers
Body: Pale yellow angora
Wing case: Pale yellow mallard flank
Hackle: Pale yellow hackle
Hook: Mustad 3906B, size 14 or 16

8.
Some Problems with Small Streams

SO FAR WE'VE suggested a good deal to indicate that small streams suffer from complex environmental problems. Aren't these small streams the basis for our large streams and rivers? If they're in trouble, then doesn't that also spell future trouble for our larger waters? Several real problems do exist with many of our small streams. All affect the quality of the water and the trout which they contain. Of course, many of the problems that small streams now harbor have been produced by man. Acid rain and dropping water levels are the indirect result of man's dominance. Three other concerns, particularly for anglers, are posted lands, overfishing, and litter. Defoliation and impoundments also harm water quality. All these concerns are serious, and we as interested small-stream fly-fishermen can do something about most of them.

Acid Rain

What does acid do to a stream? When the pH of a stream goes below 5.0, several things occur. First and most important, minerals present in the water, like iron and aluminum, attach to the gills of the trout in the stream and suffocate them. Highly acid waters can hold greater amounts of minerals in solution than waters with less acid.

Secondly, very few mayflies, and only a handful of stoneflies and caddis flies, can live in an aquatic environment with a pH lower than 5.0. Recent studies by Bill Sharpe at Penn State University show definitively a sharp drop in the number of aquatic insects as the pH of the stream decreases.

Linn Run, in southwestern Pennsylvania, runs cold and clear all summer long. This fifteen-foot-wide freestone creek stays well below 70 degrees even on hot August afternoons. Linn Run for years had an excellent reserve of native brook trout. Some small streams within a few miles of Linn Run even held good supplies of streambred rainbow trout. For years Linn Run exemplified native-trout small-stream fly-fishing at its zenith. In its magnificent setting, with the stream flowing from the Allegheny escarpment, Linn Run from all outward appearances typified top-quality eastern small-stream fly-fishing.

But Linn Run's condition has been flawed for more than a decade. This once highly productive trout fishery, and many others in the northeastern United States, has suffered from the onslaught of air pollution. Linn Run experiences severe doses of acid rain. Storms deposit highly acidic rainwater onto the Allegheny escarpment just to the east of the stream. Many of these rains carry water with pH below 5.0. The high acidity, coupled with dissolved heavy metals such as aluminum, reduce or completely wipe out the native trout population and insect life. Linn Run in the spring sometimes has a pH between 4 and 5—highly acidic—from spring rains and runoff from snowmelt. Like dozens of small streams in the Northeast that once held healthy populations of trout, the stream now possesses practically none. To many scientists acid rain, and the resultant low pH on many small streams, is the culprit.

Scientists have attacked the acid-rain problem on streams in several different ways. First they pump less acidic water from nearby wells into the acid streams to raise the pH. This works only if there is a source of water near the acid water that has a higher pH than the stream. Second, automatic devices of various types have been developed to constantly monitor and add lime as needed to the acid water to raise the pH.

Liming is only a temporary fix and is costly. If the lime-dosing device stops functioning, the stream dies. Liming works to differing degrees in countering acid-rain and mine-acid drainage. If there are too many minerals in the water—a high iron content, for example—

the metal will coat the added limestone, and liming will become ineffective.

Another recent project involving wetlands attacks the problem of dissolved heavy metals. Lloyd Stark, at Penn State University, conducts research on this approach to acid water. He and other scientists have found that various wetland plants like cattails, sedges, and others take some of the metals out of water. This water, minus some of the elements, can then be treated with lime or limestone. Under normal conditions metals in the acid water tend to clog the limestone and prevent it from neutralizing the water. With some of the metals taken out by the plant material, limestone can do its job better.

Earlier I suggested that you carry a pH-tester with you to monitor the acidity of your favorite streams. By keeping a record you can see whether the stream is improving or getting worse.

Acid Mine Drainage

Acid from sources other than rain affect small-stream fly-fishing. Coal miners destroyed many of the better streams of the early 1900s. Many of these once-exceptional trout streams will never recover from the effects of acid mine drainage. Thousands of small streams across the United States are especially affected by man's abuses. Many of these once carried good populations of native trout. Now these coffee-stained streams are completely void of any zoological form of life.

Beech Creek in north-central Pennsylvania—what a beautiful native brook trout stream this must have been at one time! The main stem and tributaries teemed with brook trout. The water falls rapidly on this cold stream in its meandering travel to the Bald Eagle Creek. But no trout live in Beech Creek any more. Mine acid decimated the fish population many years ago. Dan Shields, a small-stream afficionado, imagines that Beech Creek, if it were free from mine acid, would be one of the top freestone streams in the East. But until technology comes up with some solutions, anglers are faced with a potentially fantastic trout stream twenty miles long insidiously polluted with mine acid.

Acid mine drainage has destroyed many small streams formerly teeming with wild trout. On several trips to small streams, I've hiked up streams filled with acid drainage until I've reached an acid-free

Acid mine drainage ravages many small streams.

tributary. I know one of these well in northwestern Pennsylvania. The moment I head up this unpolluted water, I start seeing brook trout. If you find one of these unspoiled branches to a polluted stream, you can often have a spectacular day.

Look at another northeastern stream: Stony Fork Creek just south of Wellsboro, Pennsylvania. Fish the lower three miles of this pictur-esque stream, and you'll find nothing. Unrestrained mine acid flows out of an old mining shaft and pours directly into the stream at Painter Run. Fish above the Painter Run tributary, and Stony Fork teems with trout. Many areas that contain old mine shafts show similar patterns: part of the watershed—often a tributary or an upstream area—will be free of acid mine drainage. If you find one of these isolated areas, you're in for some good small-stream fly-fishing.

Overharvesting

It's easy to wipe out the trout population on a small stream. Thank-fully, the majority of you reading this book would never think of killing a trout, much less a native trout from a small stream. Neverthe-less, I've seen hundreds of small streams decimated of trout by anglers who think they have to kill their limit every time they fish. Most of the native trout caught on these small streams aren't even legal in many states. Nonetheless, greedy anglers keep these small wild trout and destroy the prospects for future fishing on many streams.

Small streams can't stand much fishing pressure. The Yellowstone, Madison, Au Sable, and Beaverkill often accommodate dozens of anglers per mile of water every day throughout the season. The small streams I write about can accept one or two anglers per mile per day—maybe once a month—and that number only if the trout are returned promptly to the water unharmed.

You'll note also throughout the book that I seldom mention any small stream by name; I do so only to make a disparaging remark about the stream. To praise a small stream in print would certainly sound the death knell for that stream.

Much of the overfishing on small streams stems from bait fishing. Bait fishing adversely affects small streams with native-trout popula-tions more than any other type of stream. Why? Many states place a minimum size on trout caught and kept. When bait fishermen fish these small streams, they unknowingly kill many of the undersized trout they return to the stream. How? They catch a lot of small trout. Often trout attack live bait like worms viciously and swallow the hook. Anglers cut the line on many of these trout. So before a bait fisherman catches his limit of, say, six trout, he might have inadvertently killed twelve other trout that swallowed his bait.

This presents a strong argument for exclusive fly-fishing on these streams. Why not set parts of small streams aside with no-kill fly-fishing-only sections? Almost always, states think of placing special regulations on large streams and rivers. Small streams and the trout they contain also need some system of protection from anglers.

Posted Lands

What a fantastic stream! Big Fill Run in central Pennsylvania contains a dozen heavy mayfly hatches. From mid-April through much of May and June, you'll find hatches and rising trout. Even the large Green Drake appear in good numbers on this diminutive stream. Every pool and productive pocket holds one or two hefty streambred brown or native brook trout. During a hatch you'll see hundreds of rising trout on the stream. Occasionally you'll hook into a trout up to twenty inches long. What a productive, spectacular small stream!

But something has happened to Big Fill recently. In the early '80s the state decided to stop stocking the stream. They rationalized that it contained a sufficient population of native trout and didn't need an overload of stocked trout. The state overlooked one important obstacle in the way of Big Fill's becoming a great wild-trout stream everyone could enjoy—access. Once the state ceased stocking Big Fill, landowners were free to post it, and now much of the lower four miles of this water is posted and not open to public fishing. Only a few select fishermen can now enjoy this impressive water.

Every day we as fishermen lose access to more and more fishing water, small streams included. Unless we react quickly and decisively, public access to fishing waters will be a thing of the past. Individuals, groups, and governments must act quickly to halt the rapid loss of access to fishing waters.

The future for small-stream fishing isn't as bleak as it is for larger waters. As we pointed out earlier, the headwaters of many of our trout

More and more streams are being posted against fishing.

streams begin and run through miles of state and federal land. Access to these will be preserved forever.

You, as an interested fisherman, must promote, support, and encourage all endeavors to enhance access to fishing waters. Work with groups like the Western Pennsylvania Conservancy and other conservancy groups. They have accomplished much to preserve and enhance our public use of lands and streams.

Contrast the access problem in the United States with New Zealand. Recently I spent a month fishing New Zealand streams and rivers. In those thirty days of fishing, I never once saw a "No Trespassing" sign. Never once in New Zealand were Mike Manfredo and I refused permission to fish any river.

Urban Sprawl and Dropping Water Levels

Have you ever revisited a small stream you haven't seen for some years? Did you notice that the water level on the stream didn't seem as high as it was ten or twenty years ago? Many small streams I've revisited seem considerably lower than in years before. Why? Look at the number of new homes placed on the watershed recently. These new homes draw on the underground water supply of the valley, and consequently the water level drops. Many of our small streams will continue to suffer a loss in volume as they continue to lose water to human consumption.

Urban sprawl has also cut into the productivity of many small streams. How many times have you revisited a small stream after a hiatus of ten or twenty years to find homes, farms, and cabins in places where wilderness once flourished? This creeping urbanization also increases fishing pressure and demands on small streams.

We have also experienced several years of severe droughts throughout the United States. I've seen some upper tributaries completely dry up or go underground during the summers of the past couple of years. Many of these had never lost their water supply completely before. On some of these small branches it will take years to repopulate them with trout—that is, if they don't continue to be intermittent with every dry season. I've fly-fished several streams that have recently gone dry. In most cases you'll find only an occasional trout that has strayed into the area.

Defoliation can also affect the water levels on these small branches and tributaries. We'll examine this later.

Warming Waters

I had fly-fished the Bald Eagle just east of Tyrone for more than twenty years. Two of its tributaries, Big Fill and Vanscoyoc runs, keep the small main stem cool. For years I could fish the Bald Eagle just below its confluence with Vanscoyoc and expect to see water temperatures in the sixties—even on the hottest summer day.

Within the past few years things have changed, and not for the better. Now temperatures in the same area register in the mid- to high seventies on hot summer days. Where brook trout once flourished, now you only find an occasional streambred brown trout. What has happened? Part of the canopy upstream was destroyed and replaced by concrete when the state built a new road. This important canopy can never be replaced.

Brook and cutthroat trout are severely limited in their range by the maximum water temperatures they can withstand. Temperatures nearing 70 degrees cause trout to migrate to cooler environs. Streams that warm above 70 degrees lose their populations of brook and cutthroat. You'll often see an intrusion of brown trout coming into an area previously populated by one of the colder-loving trout. When this occurs, it should serve as a warning sign for all anglers.

Defoliation

Beautiful, cool mountain streams predominate in many parts of the country. Recently insect infestation from oak leaf rollers and gypsy moths, and high lumber prices, have presented the problem of an open canopy. Many areas hit by the oak leaf roller, gypsy moth, and pine bark beetle have been devastated, and millions of acres have been clear-cut in all areas of the country. Still, millions more acres stand to lose their timber because of continued invasion of insects. These clear-cut sections, with no canopy to hide the stream from the sun, warm small mountain streams considerably. Waters that previously teemed with trout now abound with minnows.

Impoundments

Had you been fortunate enough to fly-fish Shavers Creek in central Pennsylvania thirty years ago, you would have found a fantastic, productive trout stream. In its upper five miles Shavers Creek harbored a good number of native brook trout. Below that, the stream contained plenty of holdovers from previous stockings and even a few streambred brown trout.

Say good-bye to an excellent trout stream forever! In the late 1950s Penn State University decided to build a dam on that stream. Since no one questioned their wisdom, they decided to use a top-release at the dam. At its deepest the dam is thirty-five to forty feet deep.

What has happened to the stream below since they constructed the dam? This once-productive trout stream now holds stocked trout for the first couple of weeks of the season. As soon as the water temperature rises above 70 degrees, the stocked trout seek out cooler tributaries. Temperatures in July and August now reach 80 degrees below the dam on this small stream. It's not uncommon to catch bass and sunfish in the stream below where once anglers caught only trout.

If only someone had urged the university to consider making the dam a little deeper and including a bottom release. As it now stands, the lower ten miles of Shavers Creek have been ruined as a cold-water stream forever because of the Stone Valley Dam. Hundreds of other cold-water streams have had or will have the same fate. We, as interested anglers and organizations, must ban these indiscriminate impoundments that alter the makeup of small streams.

Look at another example, one that shows careful planning. Codorus Creek flows into York, Pennsylvania. Several years ago Glatfelter Paper Company built a dam on the stream—with a bottom release. The water below the 125-foot-deep dam flows full and cold all summer long. Temperatures in the high fifties are not uncommon in July and August. The stream teems with trout throughout because of the cold tailwater.

On most regulated tailwaters engineers attempt to equalize volume throughout the year. Look at the Codorus in April and again in August, and you'll notice little change in the flow. Unlike other nearby freestone streams that flow with a bare trickle, the Codorus flows bank-full not only in April but also in August.

When we think of tailwater fishing, we normally think of huge western waters like the Bighorn in Montana or the Green in Utah. Small streams also benefit from a constant release of cold water from the bottom of a deep dam, however. Hundreds of these small tailwaters can be found throughout the United States.

Other impoundments, like beaver dams, can affect a small stream adversely. I had fly-fished one small stream for more than ten years. The next spring when I approached this same favorite branch, I saw a recently completed impounded area formed by several energetic beavers. For two years that dammed area produced some heavy native brook trout. By the third year, however, the beaver had taken so many softwoods out of the area that the water lacked any canopy whatsoever, and the impounded water heated up. The water temperature on the impounded area rose into the seventies by midsummer of that third year, and native trout abandoned the area.

Predation

In the past decade environmentalists have done much to save predators—at the expense of many of our native trout. Environmentalists have done much to protect the hunters but little for the hunted.

Mike O'Brien, of Williamsport, Pennsylvania, fly-fishes on a private club in the north-central part of the state. This small stream, Blockhouse Creek, joins with Texas Creek a few miles below to form Little Pine Creek. Mike likes to fly-fish after dusk, especially in July and August.

Two years ago the East was hit hard by a severe drought. Many of the small streams contained barely a trickle. Many areas of streams dried up completely. Trout died or were relegated to the remaining small deep pools. Here they became easy prey for any hungry predator. Blue herons, otter, mink, and other predators that fed on trout had a heyday. After Mike quit fishing late one night, he shined his flashlight into the deep pool he had just fished. He saw three heavy trout in the area. All three had one thing in common: they all had holes pecked in them, probably from a blue heron. All would eventually die.

Why is cover important? Why do trout hide under rocks? Why do they stay under roots of trees, undercut banks, or brush in streams?

The more cover, the better the chances of native trout to survive predators. A good stream is nothing without good cover and deep pools or pockets to protect the trout population.

We've examined plenty of problems with small streams, and we have seen that many of them are man's doing. Because man created many of these problems, man can also do something to rectify them.

9.
Improving
Fly-Fishing on
Small Streams

AFTER YOU'VE FLY-FISHED on some of your favorite small streams for a while, you'll begin questioning much of what you have done in the past. As you progress from neophyte to skilled angler, a metamorphosis occurs. This process erupts most notably after you've become an accomplished small-stream angler.

First, you begin returning all trout to their natural environs. Then, you begin speculating on how you can encourage others to do the same. Then, you begin protecting all trout on all streams as if they were your own.

As you progress, you often explore other ways you can help make the small streams you frequent even better. What about posted lands? How can polluted small streams be rehabilitated? What about returning trout? You'll concern yourself with these and other questions vital to the future of small-stream fly-fishing.

We'll explore some of the things you can do to make small-stream fly-fishing even better. We've divided the chapter into a look at fishing practices that help trout, things you can do to improve stream conditions, and things you should press the government to do.

Fishing Practices That Help Trout

What can you do to make small-stream fly-fishing even better? You can immediately help by using barbless hooks and then returning caught trout quickly and safely back to their small-stream environs. Let's look at these practices in more detail.

1. Putting them back alive

John Gordon, of Huntingdon, Pennsylvania, agreed to take me to one of his favorite trout streams. He's fished the stream for more than two decades. The state stocks the lower twenty miles of his favorite stream with a heavy number of fish. They place the majority in the stream before the season but also conduct several in-season stockings. John often avoids that stocked lower end, however, for a four-mile stretch in the headwaters that contains a mixture of streambred brown and native brook trout. In these headwaters John rarely meets another angler. John uses spinners from the opening day of the trout season until the very last day on this section of his favorite small stream.

Recently on one trip in June John caught ninety-five trout. He quickly returned all ninety-five so they could feed another day for another fisherman. Rarely does he ever keep a fish. What great trout-fishing we'd all have if all of us followed John's thinking! The only competition John has is to compare the number of trout he catches and returns with the number his son returns to the water. If John and his son killed trout on this section, how long would would it take them to decimate the population?

But is it worth returning trout? Look at what happened to me recently. Over the past ten years I have found several productive small streams and a section of a larger stream that held an unusually heavy number of trout. Almost any day I fished these waters, I had success. Nobody else seemed to fish these streams—at least no one who kept fish. Although the stream was open to any angler, it seemed as though it were my own private stream.

Recently I visited this same productive small stream and met four other fishermen, all circled around one six-foot-deep pool. When I asked them if they were having any luck, one of the four brazenly opened his creel and showed me more than his legal limit of healthy native trout. Probably in the last year I had hooked and released each and every one of these fish. Now none of them could provide sport for anyone—they were dead. How long would it take this stream to reproduce the number and size of the trout taken by these careless anglers?

I went home that evening asking myself several questions. Why don't other people release trout? Don't fishermen realize that it will take years to replace the fish? Don't some anglers realize that they can enjoy catching the same trout time and time again if they return them? On the other hand, why didn't I just keep the trout when I caught them? Hadn't I, by releasing these fish back to the water, encouraged other fishermen to overfish the stream? Hadn't I artificially kept the fish population in this stream high? I was angry, and I didn't have any answers to my questions.

Since that troubled day, I have eagerly developed the belief that if all of us want better fishing, it is our obligation to educate fellow fishermen to catch-and-release fishing.

How can we encourage anglers to return trout? Consider an experience of mine. More than twenty years ago I met Craig Hudson on a stream near Wilkes-Barre, Pennsylvania. Craig had just begun fly-fishing and had become frustrated with a mayfly hatch and rising trout that occurred just in front of him. Craig turned around, looked at me, and asked me what the trout were feeding on. I handed him two size-18 Blue Quills.

"Try these," I said. "Promise me one thing, however—if you catch any trout on these flies, please return them." Craig looked startled at my challenge to him, but he took the flies and agreed to my stipulation.

Almost immediately Craig began catching trout rising to the hatch. I watched him closely as he returned his first two to the stream. Then I walked away confident that he would return all the trout caught that day.

It was twenty years before I saw Craig Hudson again, this time on the Driftwood Branch of the Sinnemahoning Creek. I had completely forgotten who Craig was, but he remembered me. When we chatted, he recalled our first meeting twenty years before and my condition for giving him some dry flies to match the hatch.

"I haven't forgotten your precondition for giving me flies on Bowman Creek. Since that day I have not kept one trout," he said proudly. "After I returned the first couple, I felt no tinge of regret whatsoever."

Encourage all the fishermen you take with you to return their trout.

If you take anyone with you to fly-fish one of your favorite streams, do it only on the condition that he or she returns the trout to the stream. The first couple of trout they return will be the most difficult. After returning the first few, it becomes much easier.

I do plenty of guiding on eastern waters. Last year several anglers from Cleveland, Ohio, fly-fished some local small streams with me. Two of these had recently started fly-fishing. All three anglers experienced a tremendous match-the-hatch day. Green Drakes appeared all day long, and trout rose for hours. They landed many streambred browns, even a couple over fifteen inches long. On one of these occasions, one of the fly-fishers pleaded with me to keep a trout, and I asked him to return it. He finally released the fish.

Most western guides now insist that the trout caught on their guiding trips be returned. Al Troth, on the Beaverhead in Montana, has been doing this for years. These professional guides realize what catch-and-release means to the future of fishing on their streams and rivers.

Catch-and-release fishing is even more important on the small streams you might select after reading this book. Few of these streams ever see a planted trout. Once a streambred trout is killed on an unstocked small stream, it takes a long time to replace it. Constantly remind any friend you take with you of the time needed to produce another fish that size in the stream.

Until we educate enough fishermen to the wisdom of returning trout, we must rely on other measures to secure the release of caught fish. Why not encourage your state to place some sections of certain small streams aside as restricted to catch-and-release fishing? You'll see this recommendation expanded later.

It goes against the grain of most anglers to return a trout to the stream. They often strongly argue that they certainly didn't come to the stream to return fish. It's a tradition for many anglers to bring their catch home. When they arrive home, they want to show off their catch. How can you encourage them to return trout? You will see more suggestions such as conducting educational programs later in the chapter.

2. Using barbless hooks
The first few times I fly-fished a small stream with George Harvey, he admonished me for not using barbless hooks. Since that time, I

automatically take the barb off every hook, especially on these small streams where you're likely to hook a lot of small brook trout. Take the barb off the hook when you're tying the fly, or buy barbless hooks. Try to release your catch as soon as possible with little harm.

How many times did you forget to take off the barb? Many small-stream trout take the dry fly with a vengeance. Many of these same fish take the fly so deeply that it's difficult to extricate the hook from their mouth and thus many die. Using barbless hooks on small streams will help maintain the trout population. Don't begin fishing any of these streams before taking the barb off the hook.

3. Foregoing fishing small streams at certain times of the year
Rangers delay fishing on the Yellowstone River in the National Park until mid-July. Why? They allow no fishing until they feel all of the native cutthroat trout have completed their breeding cycle. This makes good sense if you want to protect future progeny. I often forego fishing small streams with good streambred brown and brook trout populations from mid-October until mid-November for the same reason. If you want to protect the future of your favorite streams, protect the breeding population and abstain from fishing when breeding commences. Rainbows and cutthroats in the West usually breed in spring, whereas brooks and browns in the East and Midwest do so in the fall.

Things You Can Do to Improve Stream Conditions

Maybe you've just begun fly-fishing small streams. You've enjoyed the experience and want to ensure a lifelong avocation. What can you as an individual do to ensure that trout-fishing in general and small-stream fly-fishing, to be specific, will be available for years to come? You have plenty of options available, including joining an organization, policing your ranks, encouraging studies on small-stream problems, and many more. Let's look at a few.

1. Joining an organization
What can you as an individual do to help preserve the future of small-stream fly-fishing? You're just one person against large companies, big landowners, and others sometimes interested in raping our lands

and waters. Certainly how you as one person feels won't count.

First, join an organization devoted to the same goals and principles that you are. Trout Unlimited, the Federation of Fly Fishermen, and the Izaak Walton League are only a few of the organizations that advocate clean streams and battle to protect our natural resources. Each of these organizations has local chapters dedicated to working on local issues. Your help can make these organizations even more effective.

There are thousands of examples where a handful of volunteers in these associations have made a difference. Just ask the Jim Zwald Chapter of Trout Unlimited, in Emporium, Pennsylvania. This group has argued for a specially regulated area on the Driftwood Branch of the Sinnemahoning Creek for years. The State Fish Commission finally granted a delayed-harvest area just north of Emporium.

Muddy Creek in York County suffers from the encroachment of man. Temperatures in parts of the stream rise well above 70 degrees in midsummer. Areas of the stream have been recently posted by landowners. The water authority devised plans to place several dams on branches of another nearby stream, Codorus Creek. One of these dams is already in place with another one planned. These dams, as planned, will doom future trout-fishing on the stream below.

John Taylor, a local outdoor writer, has pleaded with local anglers to form a watchdog organization for both streams. After many false starts, two chapters took shape. Congratulations to Jan Pickel, Jim Hershey, Steve Knopp, and other conservation-minded York County residents. After years of frustration they recently formed a Muddy Creek Chapter of Trout Unlimited and devote much of their time to the betterment of trout-fishing on that stream, ensuring fishing for future generations of anglers.

A new chapter was formed on the Codorus recently that can challenge future water-authority plans and encourage them to retain a cold-water fishery.

Look at another area, which contains no local chapter of FFF, TU, or IWL. The McConnellsburg, Pennsylvania, area possesses many fine streams in its region. Several local streams boast good hatches and a good supply of limestone-infused cold water all summer. Spring and Big Cove creeks both carry plenty of holdover trout and a great Trico hatch. Nearly all the anglers in the area, however, have been conditioned over the years to keep their catch. Few local anglers return any trout to the streams to fight for other fishermen. A local Trout Unlimited or Federation of Fly Fishermen chapter could, by example, start encouraging anglers to return some of their catch.

So joining, or better yet forming, a local chapter is just a beginning of what you can do to preserve local fly-fishing.

2. Educational programs

How can you and your anglers' group aid in accomplishing all the things we've discussed? Through educational programs, anglers can help educate other anglers. Groups and individuals interested in protecting and enhancing their environment can speak to schools, colleges, and sportsmen's clubs. They can help get the word out about the problems and challenges facing the future of good fly-fishing in the United States. At these meetings, through slide shows, speakers can show the advantages of returning fish, policing their ranks, and helping keep streams clean and open to all.

At some of the sportsmen's meetings I attend, I use a diagram showing a pool with ten trout in it. I try to demonstrate what happens if each of five different anglers fishing that pool takes a trout.

I then show another pool that also contains ten trout. But anglers who catch fish in this second pool promptly return them. This second pool, of course, will hold more trout than the one where the anglers kill fish. Even the angler in the audience who keeps every fish he catches soon gets the point when one compares the first pool to the second.

3. Adopting a stream

Some states promote adopt-a-stream programs. Local chapters of organizations become responsible for stream improvements, access, and other work important to maintaining a stream. The chapter usually meets with local authorities, and they jointly decide when, where, and what improvements are needed on a stream. Small streams not stocked by states can also be adopted and improved. In Chapter 2 we discussed some of the features of streams which contribute to good trout habitat. You may be able to construct some of those features on your favorite streams.

The Pennsylvania Fish Commission recently embarked on an adopt-a-stream program. Adopt-A-Stream in Pennsylvania encourages groups and organizations to take on a stream in their area as a project. The program on these streams includes installing appropriate stream-improvement devices. Those streams that are fortunate enough to have active Trout Unlimited or Fly Fishermen Federation groups close by have prospered. What about those thousands of wilderness streams that could benefit from stream improvements? Because many of these waters don't flow close to urban areas, they remain second-rate. On occasion you see some work done years ago under the auspices of the federal government through a grant of funds. These grants run hot and cold. Something more continuous than a grant now and then must be developed. Much in stream improvement can and should be done.

Some streams need little improvement. Many other streams, however, are not well endowed with cover and flow throughout the year. Look at your favorite streams in early May and then again in late August. You'll probably see two totally different streams—almost a Jekyll-and-Hyde character.

During April and much of May, these small streams flow bank-full, and trout have little difficulty hiding from predators. Examine the same stretch of the same stream in late August, and you will probably witness a limited flow. Where pools earlier averaged three to five feet deep, they now are barely a foot. Few large boulders rest in the water to hide trout, and brush and debris in the water in spring are now well up the bank on dry land. Trout have few places to hide and become easy prey for coons, mink, kingfishers, herons, and other birds and animals. Any trout you see in late summer scurries for cover quickly when you approach. Many small streams lack adequate holding pools to protect trout.

Now change the late-August trip to another stream where you have made some stream improvements. By tossing a rock here and a boulder there, you have added several pools. The areas dammed still hold an adequate supply of water even for large trout. When you approach, trout dart under one of the large boulders you've placed in the middle of the pool. The trout look healthy and are ready for the breeding season. After checking the rocks, you surmise that even a few more mayflies, stoneflies, and caddis flies now inhabit the improved area.

Have you thought of adding some obstacles to the stream? By just making a few improvements, you can probably bring your favorite small stream to hold more and larger trout. I have a couple of pet small streams locally. Each time I fish them, I add a couple of big boulders

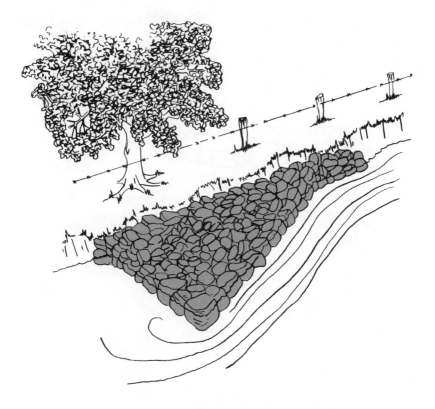

Figure 9.1
Some small streams can use stone deflectors. These devices prevent
erosion and narrow the stream channel.

here, a few rocks there, some brush at another place. Over the years,
I'm certain these meager improvements have increased the quantity
of trout in sections I've worked on. Before you do any such improvement, however, check with the landowner.

Adding improvements to your favorite small streams can make
incredible results—if the devices and improvements are well thought
out. Take, for example, Martin's Creek in eastern Pennsylvania. Look
closely at the stream, and you'll see low flow channel structures,
gabion deflectors, log frame deflectors, and other fish habitat improvement devices. We showed the results of experiments on this
stream in Chapter 3. The improvements and devices added there were

Figure 9.2
The log deflector performs the same functions as the stone deflector.

well thought out and done with the complete cooperation of the State Fish Commission. The results on this small stream were so outstanding that they need to be repeated.

Brodhead Creek lies within 100 miles of New York City. Hurricane Dianne in 1955 virtually destroyed the stream. Shortly after the catastrophe, the Corps of Engineers channelized much of the streambed to prevent future flooding. Channelizing severely reduced the reproduction of trout. Where anglers caught ten and twenty small streambred brown trout before, they now caught two and three. The Brodhead Chapter of Trout Unlimited stepped in, recognized the problem, and developed improvement devices for the channelized

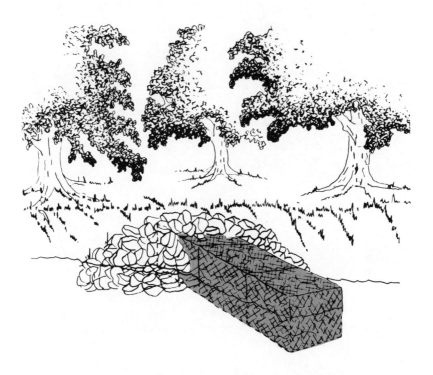

Figure 9.3
Gabion deflectors provide bank protection. Use them selectively on small streams since they often appear unaesthetic.

area. Since that time, trout reproduction in the area has been greatly enhanced.

Again, make certain before you begin making improvements on a private sector of a stream that you have the landowner's consent. If you plan to do any reconstruction, check also with your state's fisheries authority. Many of these agencies even provide you with information on types of devices and methods of installing them. Let's look at some of the improvements you can make.

Dams: If the water remains extremely cold and the stream contains a heavy canopy, adding some small dams shouldn't adversely affect temperature. Add some rocks and boulders at the tail of a pool. Note

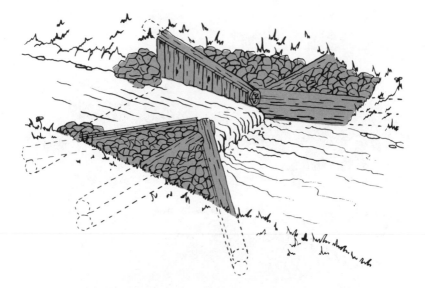

Figure 9.4
*A low flow channel structure provides a pool and cover for trout,
especially on small streams.*

how the water rises in the pool in a few minutes. You can check how much additional depth you've added to the pool; place a twig just where the water and land meet before you begin to fill in the pool. Add a couple of larger boulders in the middle of the stream to provide cover for the fish. Incorporate a couple of branches or logs on either side of the bank for additional cover. You might even add a log at the bottom of the pool and tie it in or place boulders on top of it.

Channeling: Often you'll see small streams divide and subdivide. Some water flows to the right and some to the left. If you were to channel all the flow into the left bank, it would provide enough flow to hold trout. As it is now, neither side is deep enough to hold fish. Place boulders and rocks where the water flows through on the right so most of the water flows on the left.

Garner Run experiment: For several years I've fly-fished this small stream in central Pennsylvania. Each time I leave the stream I've added a rock here, a boulder there, until after three years the complexion of the section where I've made the improvements has changed drastically. I've recorded my success over these years before and after the improvements were made.

The Pennsylvania Fish Commission publishes an excellent pamphlet entitled "Fish Habitat Improvement for Streams." This article examines many of the improvements that can be made on small streams.

4. Keeping waters open

The Whistle Pigs fly-fish on the Loyalsock and other north-central Pennsylvania streams. They have a two-week fishing holiday in early June. The group is probably the oldest organization in the country formed to further fishing. Most of the anglers live in the Harrisburg area.

One item of business each and every one of the thirty members takes seriously is attempting to keep all fishing waters in the area open to all fishermen. Posting land has been more common in the past decade than ever before. Fewer and fewer miles of fishing water are being used by more and more anglers every year. Each year at the Whistle Pigs' annual meeting, members of the club spread out onto nearby streams and meet with landowners, attempting to keeps fishing waters open to all.

What would happen to our shrinking number of fishing miles if all of us—groups, clubs, organizations, and individuals—spent a few hours each year encouraging landowners to keep their waters open to all? Overnight we'd find more water to fish.

Each Christmas week, I take gifts to some of the farmers in the area who have resisted posting their lands. What would happen if all of us treated landowners with a little more respect, kept garbage to a minimum, and showed them our gratitude with a small gift?

Private organizations like the Nature Conservancy take an active part in acquiring land. The Conservancy acquires land at the rate of 1,000 acres per day. They purchased access along the Youghiogheny River and Penns Creek in Pennsylvania.

In 1987 the Conservancy bought 1,600 acres along Colorado's Front Range. The North Fork of the Cache la Poudre River runs through Conservancy land. The Conservancy allows fishing on the river on a reservation-only basis.

Thanks to the Nature Conservancy and other organizations, sections of many streams and rivers will remain open to fishing.

5. Policing your ranks

Along all the highways of Nevada you'll encounter a sign: *Report a Poacher*. These signs encourage lawful sportsmen to report any and all poaching of game in the state, with a reward attached.

How many times have I encountered greed when fishing? I'll never forget the time I saw an angler on the far side of an eastern stream catch ten trout. He tossed all ten up on a railroad bank so he could gather them later and take them home. All were fingerlings less than six inches long. The state had recently planted thousands of fingerlings in the water. At the time this occurred, the limit on the stream was three trout over seven inches long. I finally had enough—I asked the angler how many more he planned to kill. I reminded him of the limit and size. He looked at me, mumbled some unkind words, gathered his trout, and headed back to his car. How many more trout would he have killed if I hadn't said anything?

You should be prepared to do the same. If you see an angler taking more than his limit, chastise him or at least remind him what the legal limit is. If you see him returning fish to the stream, encourage him. If you see him harvesting trout, suggest that he might return some of the fish.

Fly-fishermen are a funny lot to many other anglers. We spend an inordinate amount of money for fishing gear. We finally catch the quarry we seek, and then we promptly release it. Why did we go fishing in the first place? Wasn't it to keep trout? Or was it, more broadly, an exhilarating experience between an angler and a wary trout? The victor didn't kill the vanquished but released it to fight another day for another angler.

6. Setting an example

You'd be surprised what peer pressure can do to fellow anglers. I've seen some fly-fisherman want to keep every trout they catch. As soon as they catch a trout, they want to place it in a creel. You can show them a better way. Next time you take a friend along, show him, by example, that keeping trout is not the established norm—returning them is the accepted practice. If you return trout, others will copy your actions. Encourage newcomers to the sport to begin the day they start fly-fishing. They'll be surprised how natural it becomes to release trout.

Things You Should Press Government to Do

Anglers need support from governmental agencies to aid in small-stream improvement. As concerned fly-fishers, we should encourage these agencies to support catch-and-release and experimental areas on small streams.

1. State regulations
Let's face it: all a small stream needs is one angler who keeps trout. You can have five fishermen who return trout, but the one who keeps them can hurt the trout population.

What's needed? Later in this chapter I suggest we protect some of the smaller streams with no-kill areas. These mandatory no-kill areas succeed where voluntary catch-and-release does not.

What happens if the state won't cooperate? Maybe you can get landowners to set aside no-kill areas on their stretches. I've seen these areas posted with homemade signs telling everybody to return trout. They work in most cases. The last half-mile of Spruce Creek in central Pennsylvania contains one of these areas.

Charlie Mazza, a conservation-minded landowner, plans a no-kill stretch on the upper end of Elk Creek in central Pennsylvania. Elk is one of the top small limestone streams in the East. For more than ten years it has not had any trout stocked in it. It now totally depends on its streambred supply of brook and brown trout. Even though Elk is no longer stocked, it still gets some early fishing pressure. Many of these anglers kill trout. Charlie and adjacent landowners plan to band together to post the area as no-kill.

2. Designing experimental areas on small streams
Too often man has interfered with the work of nature. He has added stocked trout to some of the upper ends of small streams where they should not have been placed. He has added these fish on top of a good wild-trout population. Brown trout compete with and replace native

brook trout. The native brook trout population is relegated to a smaller and smaller area of a stream because of man's devastation. In addition to ill-advised stocking, man has destroyed much of the habitat for trout. He has made the water warm and more highly acidic.

Man has done much in the United States to destroy his scenic wild outdoor heritage. He must now do much to rescue and restore the outdoors. In this section we'll explore some things which can be done quickly to rehabilitate some of our lost heritage—small streams and wild trout.

First, keep areas of some small streams free of stocked trout. Most good small streams contain decent populations of native trout. If the stream contains a good supply of food for the trout, you'll find fish that grow quickly. What benefit or harm does it do to add trout to such a stream? First, stocking brings in hordes of fishermen. These anglers catch not only the stocked fish but also many of the native trout. More trout in an area than it can support with its food supply will mean that stocked fish and native trout will suffer by not growing as quickly as would be the case if only the streambred trout lived there. Additionally, the stocked population will displace some of the smaller native fish. Rather than fill a small stream with a supply of fish it can't support, the state should forego stocking and make part of the water a no-kill zone.

Second, establish no-kill areas on experimental streams. Environs of small streams are extremely fragile. Few of these waters can continue to surrender limits of trout and expect to provide recreation for other anglers. Yet there are very few no-kill sections on small streams in the United States. Most no-kill sections of which I'm aware are located on larger streams and rivers which hold more trout and a better food supply.

How will a small stream benefit from a no-kill zone? It takes years for brook trout to grow over six inches long on many of these streams. Yet many of the fish taken by anglers are the ones that lay eggs and produce future generations.

Before no-kill areas are established on small streams, however, criteria should be established. Some of those criteria should include the question of adequate food supply on the stream. Entomologists can check this easily. If you have ever checked any streams for insect life as you've fly-fished, you know you can pretty well determine the quantity of the food supply available to trout. Many of the small streams support a meager population of insects. Often you'll see native brook trout scarcely six inches long that are more than five years old in these poor-quality streams. The determining factors on many of these small streams for trout populations are the food supply and cover available to the trout. I've seen plenty of other small streams that host dozens of insects and hold well-proportioned, heavy trout. These latter streams reflect the type that might be set aside.

Third, establish no-size-limit areas. The first eight trout (or whatever the limit is) must be kept by bait fishermen. For years George Harvey and others have denounced the six- or seven-inch size limit on many small streams. They reason that bait fishermen often let the trout swallow the hook. Most of the fish affected are undersize, however. Bait fishermen, therefore, cut the hook out of the mouth, or worse yet, pull the hook out along with the guts of the fish and then release it. The trout bleeds and dies when placed back in the stream. Wouldn't it be better to make that angler using bait keep his first seven or eight fish— or whatever the limit is—rather than kill five or six trout before he catches one legal fish? How many times have you seen anglers catch trout that have swallowed the hook? How many times do these trout die?

Fourth, designate fly-fishing-only sections. Authorities have designated few small streams with fly-fishing-only sections. Rarely will you encounter a stream less than ten feet wide with such a designation. White Deer Creek in central Pennsylvania has been selected as one of the atypical small streams to have a fly-fishing-only section. Even on White Deer, however, fishermen are allowed to harvest trout after mid-June on this section. What authorities might consider on this four-mile section is to stock the lower two miles of the stream and to allow a harvest after midseason. Above that area they could establish a no-kill section.

Finally, combine these recommendations into a series of experiments. We discussed briefly our suggestion that we develop some experimental areas on some small streams to determine the effects of man on the trout population. Why not set aside certain contiguous areas on some small streams with several different sets of regulations to determine the effects of each? The following are some variables that might be studied on small streams to evaluate the effects of various types of fishing pressure. These regulations would be extremely easy to develop.

Figure 9.5
Placing boulders in small streams can provide cover for trout.

Area 1: Closed to fishing. Set aside a half mile area that would be closed to all types of fishing. Studies here could be compared with the other areas to check the effects of angling on the trout population. No stream improvements would be made to this section. This would be the control section in the experiment.

Area 2: Closed to fishing—stream improvements added. In this half-mile area, you'd see useful, worthwhile stream-improvement devices added. These devices would protect the trout and add water to certain stretches. Dams, upstream Vs and other devices, boulders, rocks, and debris could be added to make the area more hospitable to trout. Since no fishing would be allowed in Areas 1 and 2, they could compare the merit of improvement devices in one area versus none in the other. Again, since no fishing is allowed in either Area 1 or 2, these could be compared with other sections open to fishing.

Area 3: No-kill fly-fishing only. In Area 3 experts can examine the effects of catch-and-release fly-fishing. Does it have an effect on the size and numbers of trout? This half-mile section would allow fly-fishing only and could be compared to Area 1.

Area 4: No-kill—open to all types of fishing. In this half-mile section experts could look at the effects of bait fishing on released trout. Does it have a detrimental effect on the native trout population? Results from Areas 4 and 3 could be checked against Area 1.

Area 5: Regular area—no stocked trout. This half-mile section would have the same creel limit as other open streams and no restrictions on types of bait or lures. Anglers would be allowed to keep a limit of trout without any restrictions on size. This area, as with Areas 1 through 4, would depend solely on its native-trout population with no plantings of outside trout.

Area 6: Regular area—stocked trout added. Area 6 could be compared with Area 5 and others to see what effects the addition of stocked fish have on a stream. Legal-sized trout would be added on top of the native population this section holds.

Immediately someone will say that Area 1 can't be compared with Area 2. Admittedly one area will differ from another area in the types of holding water and cover. In the experiment, the group conducting the test can change Area 1 to Area 2, Area 3 to Area 4, and so on in a couple of years. After several years, the group should have a good idea of the effects of each type of fishing. If they were to conduct these types of experiments on several diverse streams, they'd have an excellent idea as to the effects various types of fishing pressure have on a stream.

3. Encouraging studies to revitalize small streams

We mentioned in Chapter 2 the studies being conducted on Linn Run and other small streams in the East. These experiments on streams with various amounts of acid from rain or coal mines attempt to rectify the conditions with crushed limestone or water from wells. Adding limestone to an acid stream neutralizes the water. I've seen small streams highly contaminated with mine acid and a pH of 4 flow with a pH of 7 to 9 below the lime-doser. For several hundred feet below the limer, particles precipitate out of the water. For a hundred yards below the limer, you'll see a repulsive stream with black goo deposited on the bottom. But the system works—and trout thrive several miles below the operation.

Scientists have approached acid streams in several ways. They

A monitoring station on Linn Run, a small stream with an acid rain problem.

attack small streams that have low pHs from acid rains with limers and wells. They drill wells near the acid-ravaged stream. The water from some of these wells produces a pH much higher (more alkaline) than the water in the nearby stream. They also combat streams contaminated with mine acid with limers and limestone.

Much has been accomplished with limestone in the Scandinavian countries. Sweden especially suffers from acid rains. In that country they spray many of their lakes with a limestone slurry. On streams affected by a low pH, they add a liming device. Some of these devices, in remote areas, work on solar power. The Living Lakes Project has done much to bring the Swedish liming technology to the United States. A simple small liming device would do wonders for many of our mine-acid and acid-rain-ravaged streams. The smaller these streams are, the easier they are to treat. And if the water quality in our small streams improves, you know the larger streams and rivers will benefit.

Another source of buffering solution for streams affected with acid pollution might be nearby drilled wells. We mentioned earlier the experiments of Linn Run and the effects of well water with a higher pH entering a fairly acid stream.

Other streams with much less of a problem might be rehabilitated by adding limestone along the banks and including limestone in cribbing and bank walls.

Each experiment in treating acid streams should be made a model so other groups interested in restoring streams can get pertinent information from it. If, on a scheduled basis, the treated areas are rotated, the experiments can be even more relevant. Experiments could be shifted from one stream to another to check their effectiveness.

All acid-abatement contraptions work on the symptoms, not on the diseases. Cease operation on a limer for just an hour, and the stream below carries highly toxic acid water which will kill trout. Thousands upon thousands of small streams can be helped with the present technology. With scientists continuing to work in this area, new methods to combat these evils will appear. New techniques for solidly sealing up old abandoned mines, new methods for attacking acid rain or eliminating it—all will appear on the horizon within the next century. Wetland experiments will devise methods of taking iron and aluminum out of acid waters.

A liming device placed on a small stream to counteract mine acid drainage.

4. Conducting base-line surveys on small and large streams

A base-line survey of a stream examines the chemical makeup of the stream along with the insects it holds. The survey measures the acidity or alkalinity of a stream, what elements it contains, and the types of insects it holds. Once a base-line survey has been established, additional surveys of the water quality of the stream can help you determine whether the water is getting worse, staying the same, or getting better. Base-line surveys can give the skilled environmentalist a quick determination of how a certain stream is withstanding the onslaught of man. Base-line surveys can help you quickly determine the status of a stream and continue to keep tabs on it. Below are some of the areas that can be covered in a base-line stream survey:

a. Altitude of stream
b. Volume and velocity
c. Alkalinity
d. pH
e. Aluminum content
f. Iron content
g. Manganese content
h. Color and turbidity
i. Water temperature
j. Air temperature
k. Bottom type (pools or riffles)
l. Insects found
m. Amount of shade
n. Aquatic vegetation
o. Substrate analysis
p. Algal abundance

If we had base-line surveys on all streams and rivers, we'd have a better idea how well our trout waters are faring. Look at the Little Juniata River as an example. For years the river contained one of the heaviest hatches of Sulphurs and Light Cahills that I have ever witnessed. Recently these hatches have waned considerably. At about the same time, the Green Drake and White Fly, both burrowing mayflies, have increased in numbers. Why? Has the bottom changed? Or is something else responsible? A base-line survey might help suggest what happened to the river in the last couple of years.

5. Eliminate electro-fishing

For years George Harvey has condemned electro-fishing, especially on small mountain streams. George and his late friend Paul Antolosky had fished many small streams a few weeks after the state completed an electro-fishing census on them. At the time, Paul Antolosky was the local waterways patrolman and saw some of the streams as they were shocked. Paul told George about the huge number of heavy brown trout the state had shocked on one such stream. A month afterwards, they traveled to the stream and fly-fished for more than a mile without catching one native fish. This is only one of many instances where George and Paul noticed a dearth of trout a few weeks after an electro-fishing episode. A recent study of the effects of electro-fishing seems to back up George's concerns, indicating that some trout show problems with backbone configuration after the event.

Sharing Small Streams with Friends

I've shared many streams with many friends over the years. I shared the Little Juniata River with a friend about two decades ago. Soon after, he shared the river with some of his friends, and on and on. Soon fishermen packed the river. All of them seemed bent on killing every fish they caught. When I first began to fly-fish the river, I could easily catch twenty to forty trout in an evening. Many of these trout measured over fifteen inches. Within a year of overfishing, even good fishermen had difficulty catching ten trout on a trip. After that first year, even the best fly-fisherman rarely caught a trout over fifteen inches long.

Sharing a small stream with a friend is even more difficult. Most of the small streams I fly-fish have one twentieth of the volume that the Little Juniata has. Experienced fishermen can literally fish them out. The real problem crops up when the friend you've taken to an outstanding small stream shares the stream with other anglers, and they with yet others—until the small stream no longer can stand the pressure.

I prize the more productive small streams I have discovered as highly as I do my grouse coverts. I share them with no one.

Summary:
The Future of Small-Stream Fishing

Many of our once-productive small trout streams now contain few trout. Streams where once George Harvey could catch more than a hundred trout a day now grudgingly surrender less than twenty. Water levels have fallen drastically in the past few decades on many of our small branches and tributaries. Acid rain has invaded many of these streams and decimated the native-trout and aquatic-insect populations. Heavy forests have given way to giant openings created by urbanization and intensive cutting. Unfavorable warm waters have replaced the once cool and pristine waters on many of our native trout streams.

Those streams that haven't been affected by acid rain and falling water levels certainly have been injured by man's greed. Anglers find these small streams and overfish them until they no longer support a great number of fish. What can be done to prevent the erosion of our last true bastion of native trout-fishing? How can you help in preserving some of these small streams and the trout they contain for future generations?

The future looks bleak for much of what we consider public fishing. Every day fishermen see more and more miles of their favorite streams posted with "No Trespassing" signs. I can show you thousands of miles of stream posted since I began fly-fishing forty years ago. George Harvey often takes me to places he hasn't fly-fished in ten or twenty years and when we reach the stream, we're greeted with these signs. The future definitely looks dismal for public access to many of our favorite trout waters.

Access to small streams, however, will continue to be much better than it is to some of our larger trout waters. Many of the headwaters of our pet streams begin and run through state forest land, state game land, national forest land, or other types of public land. These should continue to provide good small-stream fly-fishing to the angler willing to hike in to streams.

Nevertheless, we must do all we can to keep streams open to public access—even if it means turning them over to the government. The right to fish a stream should not be delegated just to the landowner but to all who want to share in the enjoyment of fishing. Individual fishermen can do more by policing their ranks and keeping these precious resources free of garbage and debris. Officials can do more by ensuring access to these cold-water streams.

Will fly-fishing small streams still be available to the next generation? Only a combined effort on the part of fishermen, landowners, organizations, and government will secure it for the future.

How can you help preserve small-stream fly-fishing for future years? By policing your ranks of anglers, encouraging others to return their catch, promoting research on acid streams, and working by every means possible to keep lands open to future fishing, you can do much. You also must become actively involved with organizations in your area that have a stake in the future of clean streams, encourage those you fish with to release trout, and advocate experiments with acid abatement and improved trout habitat.

10.
A Look at a Legend in Fly-Fishing: George Harvey

BY THE TIME he reached ten, he had torn several wet flies apart to see how they were constructed. At that time he had already fly-fished for four years. In another year he would begin a lifetime of fly-tying. He and his dad, an uncle, and several doctors regularly traveled in a Model-T from DuBois, Pennsylvania, to many of north-central Pennsylvania's top small trout streams. Now, more than seventy years later, he is regarded as the dean of fly-fishing in the United States. He's George Harvey.

Even though he's over seventy years old, George leads an extremely active life today. In an average week he ties several dozen flies, many of his own creation, coaches two or three fly-fishermen on the finer techniques of fly-fishing, autographs copies of his recently released book, *The Techniques of Trout Fishing and Fly Tying,* and fishes two or three different streams. Add to this his demonstrations and talks at fly-fishing conventions, and you can see George is a busy man.

What streams does George fly-fish? If he had his druthers, he'd fish one of the more than a hundred Pennsylvania streams that he knows like the back of his hand. Most of these are small streams. Just to fly-fish a stream with this master is an education. On an average trip, George might hike two to three miles to his favorite section on a secluded small stream.

The master, George Harvey, at work on one of the many small streams he frequents. There's no one any better than George at fly-fishing these small streams.

"I caught a seventeen-incher in that riffle there twenty years ago," George says as we hike along one of his favorite branches.

On another favorite stream you might hear him say, "I landed five trout in that pool one day thirty years ago."

George knows every productive pool and riffle on just about every small stream within a hundred-mile radius of his home and can readily direct anyone on the numerous trails and roads leading to these destinations.

What's the biggest trout George has caught on one of these small streams? He's caught streambred brown trout as large as nineteen inches long on water no wider than ten feet and brook trout in the same type of water up to sixteen inches long.

George has been fly-fishing small streams and Trico hatches for more than sixty years. He tied his first imitation of the Trico dun about 1932. He regularly fished the Trico hatches on Falling Springs in southern Pennsylvania in the early thirties, probably one of the earliest anglers to match that specific hatch.

Each May 1 to September 1, from 1937 to 1940, George did studies on Trout Run and many other streams in the Kettle Creek watershed. He researched and wrote about temperature and migration of trout on small streams. Believe it or not, George got paid for conducting those studies. What a way to earn a living! He fly-fished sections of many area small streams and tagged and numbered the trout he caught. It wasn't unusual for George to catch more than a hundred trout in a day's work. One day he caught 142 trout! On each of his days on the stream George averaged seventy trout per day.

Those days of a hundred trout have vanished along with the advent of acid rain, low water volume, and increased fishing pressure on these small streams. Seldom, except on private stretches, will you see such action. But George still vividly remembers the good old days on many of our small streams.

It's a pleasure to watch this man perform his wizardry and trickery over trout under these tightly enclosed conditions. The following are some things George Harvey does that make him an incomparable, accomplished angler in all the types of fly-fishing—and especially small-stream fly-fishing.

Fly-tying

George has developed hundreds of fly-tying innovations, more than any other fly-tier in the world. His flies are highly regarded by fellow anglers and treasured by all fly-tiers as works of art.

What are some of the innovations he's made to fly-tying? George developed a no-hackle fly back in the thirties, a huge night fly for lunker trout, the Harvey Trico, flies with fluorescent wings, and many other patterns. His book, *The Techniques of Trout Fishing and Fly Tying*, has been a bible for anglers from ages six to eighty. After seventy years of fly-tying and fly-fishing, George still creates new tying methods, new uses for materials, and new tools that benefit the fly-tier.

Look at some of the things George does when he prepares for fly-fishing on a small stream:

Maps

George carries a full complement of state forestry, U.S. Geological Survey topographic maps, and DeLorme map booklets for the entire state. He refers from one to the other to decide where to fish. George has fished almost all the small streams in his area dozens of times over his seventy-year fishing career. He still, however, remembers each road and trail near these streams—even those he may not have fished for a number of years. George also looks for tributaries and branches that leave the road. He figures that these get little or no pressure. He looks for other streams that follow almost impassable roads. I've been over potholed, rutted, boulder-strewn dirt roads that have severely tested George's Subaru and my Toyota four-wheel-drive cars.

On the stream

Once at the stream he's selected, George inspects the area to see if there's any evidence of recent fishing pressure. He looks for a path along the stream, tracks, or garbage left by recent fishermen. If George see signs of recent fishing, he often opts for another section of the stream or another stream.

Before he fishes an area, he inspects the water. Does it have some good holding pools? Are there productive pockets along the section?

Only after a short inspection does George decide to fish a stretch of water. When he does, he usually sends me downstream a half-mile. We decide when and where we'll meet. Usually we fish a new site for an hour, then get together and compare notes. Did either of us see signs of other fishermen? How many trout did I catch and miss? Were any of these trout three to four inches? These small trout give an indication as to the reproduction rate on the stream. We also ask each other if we saw many wary trout scurry from us as we hiked along the stream.

We meet after an hour; if both of us have done poorly, we leave the section for another section or another stream. If we have had a so-so day, we might continue upstream for another mile or two. If both of us have done well, we'll stay on the stream for the rest of the day. We normally don't return to the same stream within a month. Both of us agree too many trips to the same stretch might put too much pressure on the water.

Recently George and I decided to fly-fish a stream near our home. We hiked downstream two miles and walked into the stream. In the first mile, as we fished our way back upstream to the car, George and I caught a dozen streambred brown trout up to a foot long. In the second mile, neither of us caught one trout; we didn't even have a strike fishing the upper mile. What happened? George and I surmised that this upper part of the stream had dried up the year before when the East and Midwest had experienced a severe drought.

Watching George fly-fish is a real treat. Many times on isolated small streams George and I will walk along together upstream taking turns fishing productive stretches. This gives me a great opportunity to watch this dedicated master in action. George most often starts off with a black Deer-Hair Ant. He ties on a bright pink or red feather at the top of the ant so he can follow it on the shaded surface of many small mountain streams. George slams down the fly at the top of a pool and lets it ride down the riffle at the head and into the pool. When he sees the trout strike the ant, he sets the hook firmly. At seventy-nine he still has not lost any reflex action on setting the hook.

Until twenty years ago, George and his friends, Paul Antolosky, Ralph Dougherty, Don Kepler, and others, would catch a limit of small-stream trout and fry them right by the stream. George recalls many trips which ended with a fish-fry of fresh brook trout by the stream. But times have changed, and the number of native fish has decreased. In sections where thirty years ago George would pick up forty or fifty trout, he now catches a third that number. As a result of pressure and a decrease in the number of fish, George today uses only barbless hooks and returns all trout to the water promptly. Both of us agree that most of the small streams we fish can no longer stand a lot of fishing pressure, nor can they tolerate our killing a lot of the fish we catch. On many of these streams it takes several years to produce a trout comparable to the one just caught and kept.

George Harvey, the teacher

George Harvey was a professor at the Pennsylvania State University for more than thirty-seven years. He was the first to teach fly-casting and angling at the university level, beginning in 1934. His class antedated by many years any other formal college program. George taught extension courses during the late 1940s and 1950s in seventy-two different locations in Pennsylvania. He taught more than thirty-five thousand anglers in his extensive term with Penn State.

In 1960 George developed his now-famous leader formula. This leader has been the standard for three decades. He discusses his formula in *Techniques of Trout Fishing and Fly Tying*.

George still eagerly teaches casting skills and fly-tying to dozens of anglers annually. His tactics are copied by many. He helped Jimmy and Rosalynn Carter refine their fly-casting skills. He also demonstrated to them his fly-tying techniques at Camp David and accompanied them on a trip to Yellowstone Park. I learn something new from George on each trip to a small stream. He taught me the bow-and-arrow cast, how to get a drag-free float on these small streams, how to improve my roll cast, how to position myself to fish each pocket and pool on a small stream—and many other techniques. Within weeks I began to enjoy small-stream fishing and reaped the benefits of my new reservoir of knowledge by catching a good number of native trout on our trips to small streams.

Next time you're on one of your favorite streams in the Northeast and you see a truly skilled fly-fisherman teasing trout on a small stream, you, too, may be privileged to watch the wizardry of the master—one of the very few fly-fishermen who really is a legend in his own time—George Harvey.

II.
A Last Glance at Small-Stream Fly-Fishing

SO YOU'VE SAID for years that small-stream fly-fishing is not for you. You like plenty of room to cast. You delight in fishing over great hatches like the Green Drake or Western Green Drake. You want to catch lunker trout on big water. You don't enjoy crawling, creeping, or sneaking along the forest floor to catch a pint-sized streambred trout. You don't like to hike several miles into an area to fly-fish but would rather start fly-fishing as soon as you leave the car. Maybe small stream fly-fishing isn't for you.

But wait! Try small-stream fly-fishing before you condemn it to oblivion. Check one of these dwarfish streams in the middle of a hot July or August afternoon when your favorite big water lacks any decent hatch or warms near or above 70 degrees. Once you try one of these little trout streams and taste success when no one does on big streams, you'll return again and again.

Before you attempt small-stream fly-fishing, however, be prepared for it. Practice the several casts you'll need under the severely cramped conditions of a small stream. Refine your roll cast, bow-and-arrow cast, sidearm cast, and others that you'll call on under a heavy canopy and with little casting room.

Make certain that you take the proper equipment with you. Don't take a nine-foot rod and a reel with a twelve-foot leader. If you do, you'll come away completely frustrated. Be prepared for the trip with a 7- to 7½-foot fly rod like the Orvis Small Stream Special, a compatible reel, and a short tapered leader.

Be prepared for some intense action with native trout. Take plenty of terrestrials like Deer-Hair Ants, beetles, crickets, and grasshoppers with you. Take along some attractors like the Wulff Royal Coachman and the Patriot. And remember: always take plenty of patterns with you because you'll get plenty of them caught in the brush and trees. Almost every brush, bush, and tree along the stream seems to grab everything you cast.

Be prepared for the essential small-stream experience of searching for and finding excellent small streams. Take plenty of topographic maps with you. You're going to head into some new territory, and you'll have to determine where you want to fish. Look for areas of streams with few or no roads and explore—you'll find a whole new world of fly-fishing out there eager to be known. Some of these waters have not seen another angler in years.

When you're looking for new water, answer some of the questions posed in Chapter 2. Cross those streams off your list which prove to be poor, overfished, or marginal. Use some of the criteria I suggest in Chapter 2 to rate small streams. In a few years, you'll compile an impressive roster of streams on which you've had a modicum of success.

Take a friend along to enjoy the spectacular scenery, solitude, and impressive native trout you'll catch. Try two separate areas of a new stream to check whether or not it will remain on your list of favorites.

By all means, use barbless hooks on those small streams. And when you catch one of those beautiful, fighting native trout, return it to the water gently so it can provide sport and enjoyment for you or another angler later.

Please leave the small pristine stream the way you first saw it—clear of any garbage and debris. How often have I hiked into a clear mountain stream full of beautiful native trout only to see beer cans and other garbage strewn along the bank? I often carry a plastic bag with me on my trips to small streams to clean up any debris or garbage that I see along the way. Let others enjoy this clean, untouched stream and its surroundings.

Fly-fishermen, take notice! There's a whole new world out there waiting to be explored, the world of small-stream fishing. Try it, and experience the enjoyment it gives you. At first you, too, might call it fishing in a tunnel or a ditch or brush fishing. But as you progress to the stage of experts like George Harvey, you'll have a deep respect and satisfaction for the trout, scenery, solitude, and serenity you only get *Fishing Small Streams with a Fly Rod.*

Index

More from the Countryman Press
and Backcountry Publications

The Countryman Press and Backcountry Publications, long known for their fine books on the outdoors, offer a range of practical and readable manuals on fish and fishing for sportsmen and -women.

Bass Flies, Dick Stewart
Building Classic Salmon Flies, Ron Alcott
Camp and Trail Cooking Techniques, Jim Capossela
Fishing Vermont's Streams and Lakes, Peter F. Cammann
Fly Fishing with Children: A Guide for Parents, Philip Brunquell
Fly-Tying Tips, Second Edition (revised), Dick Stewart
Good Fishing in the Adirondacks, Edited by Dennis Aprill
Good Fishing in the Catskills, Second Edition (revised), Jim
    Capossela, with others
Good Fishing in Lake Ontario and Its Tributaries, Second Edition,
    (revised), Rich Giessuebel
Good Fishing in Southern New York and Long Island, Second Edition,
    (revised and expanded), Jim Capossela
Great Lakes Steelhead, Bob Linsenman and Steve Nevala
Ice Fishing: A Complete Guide...Basic to Advanced, Jim Capossela
Michigan Trout Streams: A Fly-Angler's Guide, Bob Linsenman and
    Steve Nevala
Pennsylvania Trout Streams and Their Hatches, Second Edition (revised
    and expanded), Charles Meck
Trout Streams of Southern Appalachia, Jimmy Jacobs
Ultralight Spin-Fishing, Peter F. Cammann
Universal Fly Tying Guide, Second Edition (revised) Dick Stewart
Virginia Trout Streams, Second Edition, Harry Slone

We publish many more guides to canoeing, hiking, walking, bicycling, and ski touring in New England, the Mid-Atlantic states, and the Midwest. Our books are available at bookstores, or they may be ordered directly from the publisher. For ordering information, or for a complete catalog, please contact:

The Countryman Press, c/o W.W. Norton & Company, Inc.
800 Keystone Industrial Park, Scranton, PA 18512
1-800-233-4830
http://www.wwnorton.com